BALLADS MIGRANT IN NEW ENGLAND

Ballads Migrant in New England

BY

THE COLLECTORS

Helen Hartness Flanders

AND

Marguerite Olney

WITH AN INTRODUCTION
BY ROBERT FROST

Granger Index Reprint Series

 BOOKS FOR LIBRARIES PRESS
FREEPORT, NEW YORK

LIBRARY OF CONGRESS CATALOG CARD NUMBER:

68-58825

MANUFACTURED
BY
HALLMARK LITHOGRAPHERS, INC.
IN THE U.S.A.

To my dear and sometimes helpful husband
Ralph Edward Flanders

ERRATUM

The first two paragraphs of commentary on page 244 refer to the ballad "The Schooner E. A. Horton," which ends on page 241.

CONTENTS

> *In order of appearance and with state of
> origin. Titles are those given by the singers.*

THE HEAR-SAY BALLAD

"An ordinary song or ballad that is the delight of the common people cannot fail to please all such readers as are not unqualified for the entertainment by their affectation or their ignorance."

Thus Addison with his challenge two hundred odd years ago and it might be Mrs. Flanders speaking today. We are defied not to love ballads on pain of being thought what Addison says. Balladry belongs to the none too literate and its spirit, and probably the spirit of all poetry, is safest in the keeping of the none too literate—people who know it by heart where it can weather and season properly. Ballads lead their life in the mouths and ears of men by hear-say like bluebirds and flickers in the nest holes of hollow trees. But that's no reason specimens shouldn't be brought to book now and then for sport and scholarship. We have a right to satisfy our curiosity as to what varients they may have been running wild into while our backs were turned. We can't touch their existence as a breed either to increase or destroy them. Nothing we do can. Trout have to be killed carefully so as not to exterminate them; have even to be fished out and multiplied artificially in captivity for restocking their own brooks. Ballads are different. Child hunted them, Mrs. Flanders hunts them; and they have the vitality to stay game at large, not to say gamey. You won't see the ballads of this book going back from here in print to alter the versions of the singers they were found on. No patronage of ours will smile them out of using "fee" for a rhyme word, "lily-white hands" for beauty, and lords and ladies for goodness knows what away off here three thousand miles across the ocean and after three hundred years of democracy. Their singers ought in consistency to be equally excited over the coronation and the inauguration that are in conjunction this graceful year of nineteen hundred and fifty-three.

One word more to speed the launching enterprise.

The voice and ear are left at a loss what to do with the ballad until supplied with the tune it was written to go with. That might be the definition of a true poem. A ballad does not or should not supply its own way of being uttered. For tune it depends on the music—a good set score. Unsung it stays half-lacking—as Mrs. Flanders knows full well. She has been at the same pains to recruit singers to sing the ballads for her on the stage as to collect the ballads. It is always interesting to watch how lowly the thing may lapse and still be poetry for the right people. It may flaw in meter, syntax, logic, and sense. It may seem to be going to pieces, breaking up, but it is only the voice breaks with emotion.

Robert Frost

FOREWORD

Here you will find ballads that are traditional in New England, described as a collector remembers finding them, described with backward thoughts into their origins.

I wrote the running commentary; Miss Olney transcribed the tunes from mechanical recordings made during field work.

In the experience of collectors, ballads fall as they may; singers' repertories range often from incidents buried in the past to the latest tragedy in a lumber camp . . . all cropping up with ballad trains-of-thought.

To the reader, this may be more than a book of ballads; it may prove to be a participation in prospecting for a common everyday garden variety of great literature alive today in New England.

Helen Hartness Flanders
SMILEY MANSE
Springfield,
Vermont.
1952

BALLADS MIGRANT IN NEW ENGLAND

IT IS WITH INTENTION that this book proceeds in a *"vagantes"* fashion. Only thus can any reader realize the nature of collecting traditional songs. It is no accident of planning that this book consists of music and words of ballads alternating with a running commentary. The commentary discusses the songs that follow and, it is hoped, enable the reader to share vicariously the excitement of ballad-hunting. There is always indirection, interruption to any ordered plan, when prospecting for folk ballads. That day, for instance, when on the road to an outlying village our companion remarked casually, "You know they sing while they harvest the potatoes, up on the Abrahamovich farm."

"Then why are we going in the opposite direction?" My car wheeled around even as the thought coordinated with my hands.

Or, during innumerable visits in different places, chance conversation may take this form: "I just can't remember that last verse. Aunt Winifred always could sing it straight through. She's gone now, but her daughter . . ." and a new address is set into the itinerary.

Folk ballads being migrants, so are collectors of folk ballads. But, for the sake of making available our entertaining and valuable material, we have literally stopped in our tracks, to prepare this collection for publication.

As to our tracks, some led to islands off the coast of New England, some into New York state and as many were in the heart of cities as along back-country roads in valleys or near the skyline.

Scenery could have lured us, almost as much as the "quarry." Certainly no item among the 8,000 in the Helen Hartness Flanders Folk Music Collection at Middlebury College is, to its recorders, merely words and tunes. It has the accrued associations of what the singer was told of the song, of what happened that day when the trip might have amounted to nothing, which gave such a special meaning to the piece.

"How did you know where to look for this material?"

Our earliest medium was in letters published in local newspapers. When told that old songs learned by ear were being preserved as heritage of innumerable other New Englanders, people would write a few lines of what they recalled, or give addresses of friends they knew could be helpful; or they would send

1

handwritten verses set down several generations ago in some diary, old letter, ledger, or copybook.

In 1944 I had discovered in what is known locally as South County, Rhode Island, several traditional songs which should be shared in that region. The feature editor of the *Providence Journal* welcomed the article I sent him and asked permission to send with me a photographer when next I was recording in Perryville. The combination of my story and pictures of a few singers brought on a hoard of seventy-five valuable texts and tunes from the city of Providence alone, and within the next few months over a hundred more from down near the Connecticut line.

For instance, a psychiatrist in Providence sang a graphic version of the British song of Scandinavian extraction known as "The Outlandish Knight." A Lancashire native, removed to Providence, gave us the charming "My Love Is So Pretty," sung in his family for many generations. Always the members had been told that it was composed by King Henry the Eighth. It surely might be of Elizabethan origin because of its line, "My Lord of the woolsack." In the reign of Queen Elizabeth, the wool subsidy was commemorated in that the Lord High Chancellor was thereafter, during official duties, seated on his carved wooden chair with a wool-filled sack—a woolsack—as a cushion.

Another song attributed to Lancashire, given by a Providence singer, was "Betsey, the Waiting Maid." This antique is not common to New England.

Not far from Brown University, we came upon "Gentleman Froggie," rather like the early form of the "Frog and the Mouse." This affair was bruited about in Scotland during the reign of Mary, Queen of Scots, as printed in 1549.

Some songs can be approximately dated, but we have many that puzzle even learned balladists. One, from Newport, Rhode Island, is "The Witch Song." Is there any connection between this lazy witch and the fact that in Babylon in the times of Hammurabi (1728-1686, B.C.) "a woman accused of adultery without proof might clear herself by swearing her innocence, or by ordeal by water" which "consisted of leaping into the sacred river where sinking was proof of guilt and floating of innocence."?*

We are not surprised to have in South County, Rhode Island, "James Bird,"

*Light from the Ancient Past, Jack Finegan. Princeton University Press, Princeton.

who was among the Kingston Volunteers in the Battle of Lake Erie; and a fragment of "Robert Kidd" whose treasure may be buried on nearby shores, but why should "Father Abdey's Will" be handed down in Perryville? Matthew Abdey, born in 1650, became bedmaker and sweeper at Harvard College in 1718. The will, detailing his bequests, is said to have been written by John Secomb, afterwards a settled minister at Harvard College. It was published in May, 1732, in the *Gentleman's Magazine* in this country and in England in the *London Magazine*. It is sung to the tune of "The Girl I Left Behind Me."

Near Kingston, we learned of the fitting end to "Wicked Polly," who would go to dances even though hell-fire and brimstone were to be her final lot. The itinerant preacher, Gershun Palmer, took advantage of her awful fate to warn members of his congregations wherever he orated. It was his custom, when he arrived for his scheduled appearance, to learn which members most needed which verses in the terrible and terrifying ballad; then he would stand up before them all and drive the words into their very souls.

Tenderly we hear of "The Deacon's Daughter," about Aunt Emily who caused sighs and tremors in many a withered breast, to say nothing of romantic justifications for the young, when she eloped with a man, "not her father's choice."

A region can be reborn somewhat in its flesh-and-blood survivals. "Kingston Jail" is another example. It was made up to the tune of "Nell of Narragansett Bay" by cronies of an inmate during his genial term there.

These first pages may have already given the reader more of an entrée into field work and field excitement than I had when I began in 1930. At that time I was serving on the Vermont Commission on Country Life. The Chairman of the Committee on Traditions and Ideals, Professor Arthur Wallace Peach of Norwich University, asked me to try and find very old songs known to individual Vermonters, which should be available in book form to all Vermonters.

I knew there were certain farmhouses where the past lingers into the present in haunting, indescribable fashion. Possibly it is sung by the spring water running into the barrel beside the soapstone sink, possibly it is concentrated in the timeless odors of old fabrics, worn pine floors and wide, sooty chimneys. . . .

This is a version of "Lady Isabel and the Elf-Knight," sung by Dr. Temple Burling, 100 North Main Street, Providence, Rhode Island. He says: "I heard this sung in Iowa, and I once heard a sea chantey sung to the same tune."

H. H. F., Collector
January 22, 1945

THE FALSE-HEARTED KNIGHT

(Child 4)

Come listen, come listen, my good people all;
Come listen awhile unto me,
Of the false-hearted knight and the little Golden,
The truth unto you I will sing, sing, sing;
The truth unto you I will sing.

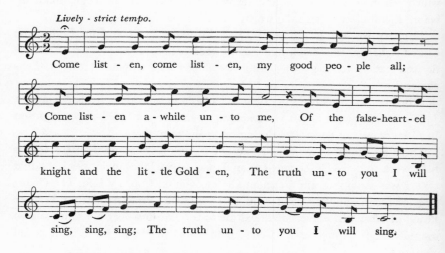

Lively - strict tempo.

Come list-en, come list-en, my good peo-ple all; Come list-en a-while un-to me, Of the false-heart-ed knight and the lit-tle Gold-en, The truth un-to you I will sing, sing, sing; The truth un-to you I will sing.

He followed* her up, he followed her down;
He followed her to her bed chamber side.
She had not the wings to fly away from him
Nor the tongue to tell† him "O nay!", "O nay!", "O nay!"
Nor the tongue to tell him "O nay!"

---

* "Follered" in a copy of the words sent by mail December 4, 1944.
† "Say" in words sent by mail.

And come along with me,
And I'll take you to old Scotland
And there I'll marry thee."
"Oh, get you up, my little Golden,

(*Follow pattern*)

"O take of your father's yellow-beating gold,
Likewise of your mother's fee,
And the two best horses in your father's stable,
Where they stand, thirty and three." etc.

She took of her father's yellow beating gold,
Likewise of her mother's fee,
And the two best horses in her father's stable,
Where they stand, thirty and three. etc.

He mounted on the bonny, bonny brown,
And she on the dappl' and gray,
And they rode till they came to the sea-beating shore,
Three long hours before it was day. etc.

"O get you down, my little Golden,
And come along with me.
Six king's daughters have I drownded here,
And the seventh you air for to be. etc.

"Take off, take off that gown so fine
And deliver it unto me,
For it is not meet that so costly a thing
Should rot in this wat'ry tomb. etc.

"Take off, take off those shoes so fine
And deliver them unto me.
For it is not meet that so costly a thing
Should rot in this wat'ry tomb. etc.

"Take off, take off those hose* so fine
And deliver them unto me,
For it is not meet that so costly a thing
Should rot in this wat'ry tomb. etc.

"Take off, take off that smock so fine
And deliver it unto me,
For it is not meet that so costly a thing
Should rot in this wat'ry tomb." etc.

"O turn you all around and about
And gaze on the leaves of the tree,
For it is not meet that a villain like thou
A woman unclad should see." etc.

He turned him all around and about
And gazed on the leaves of the tree.
She catched him 'round his middle so small
And tumbled him into the sea. etc.

"Lie there, lie there, thou false-hearted knight,
Lie there instead of me.
Six king's daughters have you drownded here,
But the seventh hath drownded thee." etc.

She mounted on the bonny, bonny brown,
Led home the dappl' and gray,
And she rode till she came to her father's stable,
Three long hours before it was day. etc.

It's up speaks the pirate then
To the Golden and did say,
"O my little Golden, it's where have you been,
So long before it was day?" etc.

"Oh, hold your tongue, my pretty pirate,
And tell no tales on me,

---

* "Stockings" in words sent by mail.

And your cage shall be lined with yellow beating gold
And hung on yon willow tree." etc.

It's up speaks the father then
To the pirate and did say
"O my pretty pirate, why are you prattling
So long before it is day?" etc.

"Oh, I dreamed seven cats came to my cage door
And said that they would eat me,
And I was calling my little Golden
To drive those cats all away." etc.

Sung by Mr. John C. Hall, 73 Holden Street, Providence 8, Rhode Island. Mr. Hall wrote that this song was popular during the reign of Henry VIII and says that it is reputed to have been written by Henry VIII himself. He writes: "I have never seen the song in print. It was handed down from one generation to another, in England, where I learned it. I remember our minister changing one of the lines, when we used to get together for a few songs.

H. H. F. and M. Olney, Collectors
Early 1945

MY LOVE IS SO PRETTY

My love is so pretty,
So lively, so witty,
None in town or in city
Her hand would disgrace.
My lord of the woolsack
His coachman would pull back
To get a look full smack
At her pretty face.

CHORUS

With a fol di dol la diddy,
Fol de dol la diddy,
Fol di dol la diddy,
Fol di dol day.

She's young and she's tender;
She's tall and she's slender,
As straight as a fender,
From top to her toe.
Eyes like stars glittering,
Mouth always twittering,
Fingers to fit a ring
Ne'er were made so.

Moderately fast.

My love is so pret - ty, so live - ly so

wit - ty, None in town or in cit - y her hand would dis -

grace, My lord of the wool - sack, his coach-man would pull back

To get a look full smack at her pret - ty face. With a

fol - di - dol la - did - dy, lol - di - dol la - did - dy,

Fol - di - dol la - did - dy, fol - di - dol - day.

Remaining verses:

(as above)

CHORUS

Head like a holly bower,
Cheeks like a cauliflower,
Nose like a jolly tar (tower)
By the sea shore.

Then haste, O ye days and nights,
That I may taste delights,
And with church holy rites
Make her my bride.

CHORUS

On the record Mr. Hall states: "My name is John Hall. I was born in Lancashire, England and I learned this song from my grandfather, John Barrie, who would have been over a hundred years old were he living today."

As sent by Mrs. Evelyn W. Braids, 885 Hope Street, Providence, Rhode Island. Mrs. Braids writes: "My mother passed on in 1925 at the age of 97 years and 3 months . . . and I have heard her sing these songs many times, tho' I have never seen the music."

H. H. F., Collector
May 7, 1945

BETSEY

(Betsey, the Waiting Maid)

Oh, Betsey was a lady fair;
She'd just returned from Lancashire,
Bound out, a servant for to be,
But fitted for some higher degree.

Her mistress had one only son.
'Twas his affections she had won.
'Twas Betsey's beauty shone so clear,
That drew his heart into a snare.

"Oh, Betsey, Betsey, I love you well;
I love you better than tongue can tell.
I love you as well as I love my life,
And I intend to make you my wife."

Oh, Bet-sey was a lad-y fair; She'd just re-turned from Lan-ca-shire, Bound out, a ser-vant for to be, But fit-ted for some high-er de-gree.

His mother, being in the other room,
She heard these words come from her son,
And she resolved all in her mind
To break up all her son's designs.

So the next morning she arose,
Saying, "Betsey, Betsey, put on your clothes;
Put on your clothes and with me go
To wait on me a day or so."

She dressed herself in rich array
And she and her mistress strolled away
Where a ship lay murmuring all in the sound,
Saying, "For Virginia poor Betsey's bound."

Oh, when his mother return-ed home,
She found her son there all alone.
"You're welcome home, mama," he cried,
"But where is Betsey, the servant maid?"

"Oh, son, oh, son, oh, son," said she,
"Would you marry a maid of low degree?
I'd rather see you now lie dead
Than to marry Betsey, the servant maid."

Soon after that he took sick in bed
With dreadful pains all in his head.
In slumbering dreams you might hear him sigh,
Saying, "Now for Betsey I shall die."

And when she saw her son lie dead,
She wrung her hands and weeping said,
"If I could see my son live again,
I'd send for Betsey o'er the main."

Sung by Mrs. E. E. Hills of Providence, Rhode Island, as learned from her mother when a child.

H. H. F., Collector
January 22, 1945

GENTLEMAN FROGGIE

A frog went a-courting; he did ride
   Mm-hmm
A frog went a-courting; he did ride
With sword and pistol by his side
   Mm-hmm.

And when he came to Miss Mousie's hall,
He gave a loud knock and he gave a loud call.

"O Mistress Mouse, are you within?"
"O yes, kind sir, I'm sitting to spin."

He took Miss Mousie on his knee
And says, "Miss Mouse, will you marry me?"

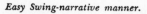

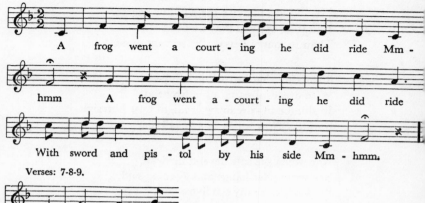

Easy Swing-narrative manner.

A frog went a court-ing he did ride Mm-
hmm A frog went a-court-ing he did ride
With sword and pis-tol by his side Mm-hmm.

Verses: 7-8-9.

(follow the above pattern)

"O not without Uncle Rat's consent
Would I marry the Pres-eye-dent!

"O Uncle Rat has gone to town
To buy his niece a wedding gown."

"And where shall the wedding be?"
"In a great big hole in a great big tree."

"And what shall the bride have to wear?"
"A white silk dress and a rose in her hair."

"And what shall the bride have to eat?"
"A piece of bread and a piece of meat."

"And what shall the wedding supper be?"
"Two white beans and a black-eyed pea,"

They took a sail upon the lake
And were all gobbled up by a big black snake

Mrs. William J. Bloomfield of Newport, Rhode Island, says this song is a fragment "sung by my aunt eighty years ago." The tune seems a variant of Mrs. Sullivan's "Kathleen."*

M. Olney, Collector
December 5, 1945

THE DROWNING LADY

(The Witch Song)

She bobbed it up, she bobbed it down,
She bobbed it to the brim,
But he with his walking-stick,
He bobbed her farther in.

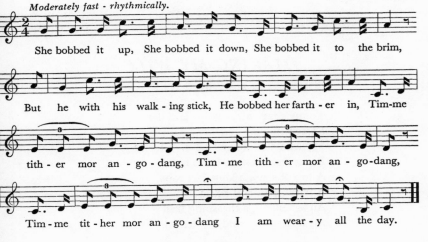

Moderately fast - rhythmically.

She bobbed it up, She bobbed it down, She bobbed it to the brim,

But he with his walk-ing stick, He bobbed her farth-er in, Tim-me

tith-er mor an-go-dang, Tim-me tith-er mor an-go-dang,

Tim-me tith-er mor an-go-dang I am wear-y all the day.

Tim me tither morango-dang
Tim me tither morango-dang
Tim me tither morango-dang
I am weary all the day.

So now my song is ended,
And I can sing no more.

* Published in *The New Green Mountain Songster*, Yale University Press, New Haven, p. 41.

But wasn't she the lazy witch
That wouldn't swim to the shore?

REFRAIN:

Excerpt from Witchcraft in Old and New England *by George Lyman Kittredge, Harvar*
University Press, Cambridge, p. 29: "An actual case of the kind, from the ninth or ten
century, is recorded (along with the witch's punishment by drowning) in an account
the title to a piece of land in Northamptonshire."

As sung by Mr. William H. Webster of Wakefield, Rhode Island. This was one of h
grandfather's songs.

H. H. F., Collect
May 6, 1945

MAKING MY WILL

(Father Abdey's Will)

To my dear wife, my joy and life
I freely now do give her
My whole estate and all my plate,
Being just about to leave her.
A tub of soap, a long cart rope,
A frying pan and kettle,
An ashes pail, a thrashing frail
An iron wedge and beetle.

Two patent chairs, nine worden pairs,
A large old dripping platter,
The bed of hay on which I lay,
An old sauce pan for batter,
A little mug, a tin quart jug,
A bottle full of brandy,
A looking glass to see your face;
You will find it very handy.

A musket true as ever flew,
A pound of shot and wallet,
A leather sash, my calabash,
A powder horn and bullet.
An old sword blade, a garden spade,
A hoe, a rake, and ladder,
A wooden can, a close stool pan,
A clister pipe and bladder,

Sprightly-strict tempo.

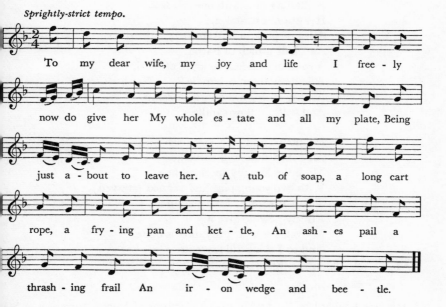

To my dear wife, my joy and life I free - ly
now do give her My whole es - tate and all my plate, Being
just a - bout to leave her. A tub of soap, a long cart
rope, a fry - ing pan and ket - tle, An ash - es pail a
thrash - ing frail An ir - on wedge and bee - tle.

A greasy hat, my old tom cat,
A yard and half of linen,
A woolen fleece, a pot of grease,
In order for your spinning.
A small-tooth comb, an ashen broom,
A candle stick and hatchet,
A coverlet striped down with red,
A bag of rags to patch it.

A ragged mat, a tub of fat,
A book put out by Bunyan,
Another book by Robbin Cook,
A skein or two of spun yarn,
An old black muff, some garden stuff,
A quantity of borage,
Some devil's weed,* some burdock seed
To season well your porridge.

A chaffing dish with one salt fish,
If I am not mistaken;
A leg of pork, a broken fork,
And half a flich of bacon.
A spinning wheel, one peck of meal,
A knife without a handle,
A rusty lamp, two quarts of ramp,
And half a tallow candle.

My pouch and pipe, two oxen's tripe,
An oaken dish well carved,
My little dog, my speckled hog,
With two young pigs just weaned (starved).
This is my store; I have no more.
I freely now do give it.
My years is spent; my days is done,
And so I think I'll leave it.

* In recording this is sung "devil's seed."

A fragment furnished by Dr. Lucille Palmer, Professor of Modern Languages at State
College, Kingston, Rhode Island.

H. H. F., Collecte
January, 1945

BOLD KIDD, THE PIRATE

'Twas the (8th, 12th?) of October
We set out to sea.
(Two lines here, I think.)

We'd not been sailing one day
Or two days, or three,
When the watch in the mizzen (?)
A strange sail did see.

With emotion.

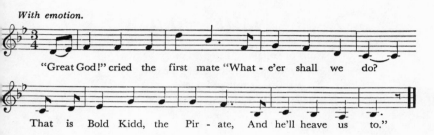

"Great God!" cried the first mate "What - e'er shall we do?

That is Bold Kidd, the Pir - ate, And he'll heave us to."

....
....

And from her . . ? . sail,
Skull-crossbones did fly.
(Or: The flag on her tops'l
     Skull crossbones did fly.)

"Great God," cried the first mate (?)
"Whate'er shall we do?
That is Bold Kidd, the Pirate,
And he'll (she'll) heave us to."

(Dialogue here between members of the crew.)

"Oh, no," cried the captain,
"That ne'er shall be so;
We'll N? . . the top d'gansail (?)
And from her we'll go."

She chased us all night, boys,
And part of next day;
Then she pulled in her spanker,
And fared (sailed?) far away.

Sung by Mr. William Webster, at the Perryville Grange, Tuckertown, Rhode Island, learned from his father.

H. H. F., Collec
October 24, 1944

JAMES BIRD

Sons of freedom, listen to me,
And your daughters, too, give ear;
To a sad and mournful story
As was ever told shall hear

Declamatory manner.

Sons of free-dom list-en to me
And you daugh-ters too give ear To a sad and mourn-ful
sto-ry As was ev-er told shall hear.

Hull, you know, his troops surrendered,
And defenseless left the West.
There our forces quickly assembled
The invaders to resist.

Amongst the troops that marched to Erie
Was the Kingston volunteers.
Captain Thomas them commanded
To protect her West frontiers.

Tender were the scenes of parting.
Mothers wrang their hands and cried.

Maidens wept their swains in secret.
Fathers tried their hearts to hide.

But there is one amongst the number
Tall and graceful in his miens;
Firm his step, his looks undaunted;
Scarce a nobler youth you've seen.

One sweet kiss he snatched from Mary,
Craved his mother's hand once more;
Pressed his father's hand and left them
For Lake Erie's distant shore.

Mary tried to say, "Farewell, James,"
Moved her hands, but nothing spoke.
"Good-bye, Bird, may heaven protect you."
From the rest at parting broke.

Soon he came where noble Perry
Had assembled all his fleet.
There the gallant Bird enlisted
Hoping soon the foe to meet.

Where is Bird? The battle rages.
Is he in the strife or no?
Now the cannon roars tremendious.
Dare he meet the hostile foe?

Ah! Behold him! See him, Perry!
On the selfsame ship they fight.
Though his comrades fall around him,
Nothing can his soul affright.

But behold! A ball has struck him.
See the crimson current flow!
"Leave the deck," exclaimed great Perry.
"No," cried Bird, "I will not go.

"Here on deck I took my station.
Ne'er will Bird his colors fly.
I stand by you, gallant Captain,
Till we conquer or we die."

Still he fought, though faint and bleeding,
Till our stars and stripes arose,
Victory having crowned our efforts,
All triumphant o'er our foes.

And did Bird receive a pension?
Was he to his friends restored?
No, nor never to his bosom
Clasped the maid his heart adored.

But there came most dismal tidings
From Lake Erie's distant shore.
Better if Bird had perished
In the battle's awful roar.

"Dearest parents," said the letter,
"This will bring sad news to you.
Do not mourn your first beloved,
Though this brings this last adieu.

"I must suffer for deserting
From the Brig Niagara.
Read this letter, brother, sisters;
'Tis the last you'll hear from me."

Sad and gloomy was the morning
Bird was ordered out to die.
Where the breast not dead to pity
But for him would heave a sigh?

See him march and bear his fetters.
Harsh they clink upon the ear.

But his step is strong and manly
For his heart ne'er harbored fears.

Though he fought so brave at Erie,
Freely bled and nobly dared,
Let his courage plead for mercy;
Let his precious life be spared!

See him kneel upon his coffin.
Sure his death can do no good.
Spare him! Hark! Oh, God, they've shot him!
See his bosom streams with blood.

Farewell, Bird, farewell forever.
Friends and home you'll see no more,
For your mangled corpse lies buried
On Lake Erie's distant shore.

clergyman of the church in Kingston, Rhode Island, Gershun Palmer, at the age of
inety-two, used this song as a solo at the commencement of meeting when he preached
nce a month in Kingston, as well as on his sixty-mile circuit. He did not compose the
ords nor the tune. This was recollected by Mrs. Carder Whaley, in Perryville, Rhode
sland. She called it her grandmother's song and had been told it was sung in churches
› show the sin of going to dances. The tune has been handed down in the Whaley family
om one generation to another. A version of this song, as known in the Knowles family
f Wakefield, Rhode Island, was published by John D. Swain in the April, 1907, issue
f the *New England Magazine*.

H. H. F., Collector
October 24, 1944

WICKED POLLY

Young people, hark while I relate
The story of poor Polly's fate.
She was a lady young and fair
And died a-groaning in despair.

To balls and parties she would go
In spite of all her friends could do.
"I'll turn," said she, "when I am old
And God will then receive my soul."

One Friday morning she fell sick.
Her stubborn heart began to quake.
She cried, "Alas, my days are spent.
It is too late now to repent."

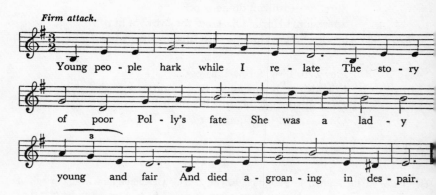

Firm attack.

Young people hark while I relate The story of poor Polly's fate She was a lady young and fair And died a-groaning in despair.

She called her mother to her bed.
Her eyes were rolling in her head.
A ghastly look she did assume.
She cried, "Alas, I am undone.

"My loving father, you I leave.
For wicked Polly do not grieve,
For I must burn forever more
When thousand thousand years are o'er.

"Your counsels I have slighted all
My carnal appetite to fill.
When I am dead, remember well
Your wicked Polly groans in Hell."

She wrung her hands and groaned and cried
And gnawed her tongue before she died.
Her nails turned black, her voice did fail.
She died and left this lower vale.

May this a warning be to those
That love the ways that Polly chose.
Turn from your sins, lest you like her
Shall leave this world in black despair.

first heard this sung in Perryville, Rhode Island, by Mrs. Mary Fitzgerald. Later it was
rnished by Mrs. Edna Hewitt Tryon of North Stonington, Connecticut, who wrote:
[am familiar with the verses, for father often told the story of the elopement and
ɹoted them to us. I believe they were composed by a shoemaker, crippled but of a
mble mind who lived across our street, Wheeler Hakes by name. My father was a small
ᵒy at the time of 'false-hearted' Emily's escapade, and heard much about it and the
ɛtails were impressed on his little boy mind, especially as he found out that his father
aned the 'blacksmith' his horse to make the getaway. In my youth, I knew both the
˙ide and groom of the poem, not an especially romantic couple then, but always inter-
ting to me because of the story."

H. H. F., Collector
Early 1945

THE DEACON'S DAUGHTER

In Shonnuck there lived a lady so bright.
A Deacon's fair daughter, his own heart's delight.
For oh! she was handsome, both charming and neat,
But her heart, it was treacherous and full of deceit.

A young man he courted her, a gay gallant youth,
Who was much respected for fame and for truth.
He courted this damsel; 'twas known far and wide
That it was his intentions to make her his bride.

The day was appointed; each had a new dress,
And they being published, invited their guests.

Oh, young man, be careful; be courteous and wise,
For there's sad disappointments in many a prize.

In the middle of the night, when her parents were asleep,
This false-hearted lady from the window did creep.
All things being ready, the plot was all laid.
There stood her young gallant, a blacksmith by trade.

Easy swing.

In Shon-nuck there lived a lad-y so bright A dea-con's fair daugh-ter his own heart's de-light. For oh! she was hand-some both charm-ing and neat, But her heart it was treach-er-ous and full of de-ceit.

Var:

Verses 3   point - ed;   each
       5   wag - on;   a -
       8   man being de-

Then into the wagon; away they both flew,
For the wicked will flee when there's none to pursue.
She left her dear parents, their houses and land,
And on the next day gave that blacksmith her hand.

Her parents being pious, they both loved the Lord.
They were followers of Jesus, believed in his words.
Straight 'way to their closets they both did repair
And poured out their hearts to their Saviour in prayer.

When Jesus our Saviour the last trum' shall sound,
And myriads of angels attending Him down.
He'll call home his people whom earth now despise
And in mercy will wipe all their tears from their eyes.

And now this young man, being deprived of his bride,
"Oh, false-hearted lady," in pity he cried.
"May God grant you pardon for the false oath you swore,
So farewell, false-hearted Emily, farewell forever more."

ıng by Dr. David Matteson, Box 63, Lafayette, Rhode Island, and introduced to H. H. F.
ᵧ Mr. William Webster of Perryville, Tuckertown Road, Rhode Island.

H. H. F., Collector
May 8, 1945

OLD KINGSTON JAIL

Give kind attention, one and all,
And listen to my tale.
I will warble you a ditty
About the crooks at Kingston Jail.
I know it will amuse you
To hear about the stars
And the doing time at Kingston Jail
Behind those iron bars.

CHORUS:

It's old Kingston Jail,
We're longing for the time
For Wilcox to unlock the doors
And tell us all to climb.
We'll jump into our hats and coats
And travel off by rail
And bid farewell to the white-washed cell
We had at Kingston Jail.

How well do I remember
The night they took me in;
The night I sampled corn juice
Enough to make me sing,
And they passed me out a banjo
While at it I did sail,
And we had a regular jubilee
That night in Kingston Jail.

CHORUS.

Let's keep the banjo singing,
It makes us feel so well.
A happier set of convicts
Had never graced a cell,
And we wake up in the morning
To eat our toasted quail,
And we'll all have indigestion
If we don't leave Kingston Jail.

CHORUS.

There were three jolly forgers
As ever drove a quill.
Sorrow never visits them;
They always eat their fill.
There's Watson, Smith, and Burdick,
Who would not ask for bail,
And swore they'd leave the Dixon House,
To dwell in Kingston Jail.

CHORUS.

There's Poley, an honest looking chap,
As you'd meet in many a day.
He's worked from San Francisco
To Narragansett Bay.

He's done his time at Whethersfield;
Old Auburn he has seen,
And he robbed that contribution box,
That slippery Hiram Green.

CHORUS.

There is Tommy Rolby,
From Italy sunny clime,
With blacky eyes and blacky hair;
It sparkles all the time.
He thinks of his loving damsel
That awaits him at Peace Dale
And swears he'll squeeze her 'most to death
When he gets out of jail.

CHORUS.

Now my song is ended,
In confidence to you;
Before I go any further,
I'll bid you all adieu.
As I cast my eye around me,
I see your features pale,
And if some of you had your just due,
You'd be in Kingston Jail.

LAST CHORUS:

It's old Kingston Jail,
We're longing for the time,
For Wilcox to unlock the doors
And tell us all to climb.
Then straightaway rush for Webster's
And merrily tell the tale,
And with him drink John Wilcox drunk,
That keeps old Kingston Jail.

. . . Enter any such home. Bookshelves, and every farmhouse has its boo
shelves, even now are likely to contain volumes whose imprints are arou
1800. There will be histories, biographies, essays, tales of adventure, Shake
peare's works, "Pilgrim's Progress," and Watt's "Hymns." Along with the
are poems, orations, travels and history, sometimes in their original Roman
Greek (as Boswell will have it). On the parlor table will be the family Bibl

Family records of undistinguished, as well as distinguished lives, show th
a goodly proportion of the men folks left the land only during their educatic
in a nearby college, or for the seasonal driving of stock or poultry for slaught
and sale in the nearest market. But the men returned home to more tha
chores, scenery, friendships, religious meetings, and the occasional kitche
"junkets." They had a relish for good literature. Biography, romances, histor
and legends, and the classics were theirs by heredity or by adoption.

This during my lifetime in Vermont, I knew. I did not know that t
heredity or adoption they possessed an unwritten lore—ballads passed alor
by word of mouth during many generations of memories. Sea battles, bord
frays, chronicles, tavern songs, pioneer tragedies and the like, were learne
"by ear," *in their tune.*

It should be mentioned that if the transcriptions in this book are not i
every case consistent with the accompanying verses, it may be prompted t
the fact that the singer did not always record for us the entire ballad.

In my earliest field trips about the state, I came upon remnants of an or
tradition from the time of the skalds to the present, records of periods, peopl
and locales as diverting and as entertaining as foreign travel. Most histori
never mention what many early Americans retained from a storied past. Bu
I found out. After some twenty years of going up and down this northeaster
land of ballads, there are hundreds of byroads that have some associatio
hundreds of noncommittal doorways which, opened by perfect strangers, hav
given momentous experiences in texts and tunes. There are the crossroad
near a covered bridge at the North Village. Take the turn to the left. At th
first farm you can hear "Little Harry Huston" sung most tenderly as it ha
been handed down from Irish forebears. Actually, it is the old tale spoken o
in the Annals of Waverly (a monastic chronicle from the reign of Henry II
1216-1257,) under the year 1255—old when Chaucer included it as "Th
Prioress' Tale." If any reader has been looking ahead, he may wonder wh

e subtitle given to "Little Harry Huston" is "Child 155." If he is among
e uninitiated he should be told that Professor Francis James Child was the
utstanding scholar who brought traditional British ballads into range for
omparative study by anthropologists, by the scholars of many countries in
e humanities, as well as by social scientists. He assembled the variants of
05 antique ballads found in manuscript and printed collections which com-
rise a monumental work of five volumes. Each ballad has since been known
y the number it was given in his collection. This was highly necessary because
ames in ballads alter down the generations, as readily as in a game of
gossip." For instance the original title for Child 155 was "Sir Hugh, Or The
w's Daughter."

The late Professor George Lyman Kittredge performed a very special service
ballad lovers in compiling from the 305 items an abridged edition.

Now let us proceed further up the road. Some fourteen miles away, on
hrewsbury Mountain is another singer who presents a form of the White
aternoster, mentioned by the carpenter in "The Miller's Tale."

When the children of the general storekeeper ask for the "Cabbage and
Teat song," what do they get? They hear a *cantefable* directly descended from
a Arthurian legend, but also closely related to the Canterbury tale, "The
Vife Of Bath." Now it is called "The Half-Hitch." It is full of bold and bald
umor, both spoken and sung.

Or, at a covered bridge, take the *right-hand* turn. When you come to the
armhouse backed up against the mountain, with a far wide view of the
Iack River Valley from under its porchbrows, turn into the dooryard. You
an hear, in that home, a version of "Lord Randall" in an unusually narrative
ane (bequeathed with a "down, derry-down" chorus), "The Black Water
ide," "The Dark-Eyed Sailor,"* and many more with lines that are arresting
s literature. . . .

---

* Published in *The New Green Mountain Songster,* p. 36.

In North Springfield, Vermont, Mrs. John Fairbanks sang this song as learned from h
mother, Margaret Kelley, of County Limerick, Ireland, who learned it from her peopl
H. H. F., Collect
September 29, 19

LITTLE HARRY HUSTON

(Child 155)

Yesterday was a very fine day,
The finest day in the year, year,
When little Harry Huston and schoolboys all
Went out to play at ball, ball,
Went out to play at ball.

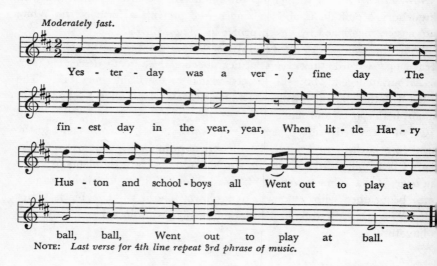

Moderately fast.

Yes - ter - day was a ver - y fine day The fin - est day in the year, year, When lit - tle Har - ry Hus - ton and school - boys all Went out to play at ball, ball, Went out to play at ball.

NOTE: *Last verse for 4th line repeat 3rd phrase of music.*

The first little tip Harry Huston gave the ball,
It was not good at all, all,
The second little tip Harry Huston gave,
He broke the window all, all,
He broke the window all.

A Jewess, she came down the stairs
And she all dressed in green, green,
Saying, "Little Harry Huston, if you come here"
....
....

"I'll not go back, and I won't go back
And I'll not go back at all, all,
For if my mama came to know
She would" ....
....

She coaxed him back with an apple so red
And with a cherry so sweet, sweet,
And took him to her own dressing room
Where she slew him like a sheep, sheep,
Where she slew him like a sheep.

She rolled him up in a winding sheet,
It was her own winding sheet, sheet,
And she took him to Saint Simon's well
Which was seven fathoms deep, deep,
Which was seven fathoms deep.

Five o'clock was past and gone,
And all schoolboys gone home, home.
Every mama had her boy
Harry Huston's mama had none, none,
Harry Huston's mama had none.

When she went to the Jewess' house
And kneels down on a stone, stone,
Saying, "Little Harry Huston, if you be there,
Will you pity your mama's moan, moan,
Will you pity your mama's moan?"

"He is not here, nor he was not here
And he's not been here all day, day,
But if you go to Saint Simon's well
You might have seen him there, there,
You might have seen him there."

She went unto Saint Simon's Well
And knelt down on a stone, stone,
Saying, "Little Harry Huston, if you be there,
Will you pity your mama's moan, moan,
Will you pity your mama's moan?"

"How can I pity your moan, mama,
When I am here so long, long,
The little pen-knife she stuck through my heart;
The Jewess, she did me wrong, wrong,
The Jewess, she did me wrong.

"But come tonight at twelve o'clock
And there you'll see my ghost, ghost;
Place my schoolbooks at my feet
And my Bible at my head
That my schoolmates they may read, read,
That my schoolmates they may read."

Harry C. Ridlon of Bennington, Vermont, who formerly lived near Shrewsbury Mountain, Vermont, writes: "The above was sung to me in childhood as I was taught to call the four high posts of the old 'four-poster' bed—Matthew, Mark, Luke and John. It had mostly escaped my memory, but I recently acquired a version from the Kentucky Mountains as collected and sung by John Jacob Niles. Mr. Niles says that it is an old Elizabethan carol brought to this country and still sung in the remote Southern districts."

H. H. F., Collector
November 25, 1942

WHITE PATERNOSTER
MATTHEW, MARK, LUKE, AND JOHN

Matthew, Mark, Luke and John,
Bless the bed that I lie on.
Four bright angels at my bed,
Two to the bottom and two to the head,
Two to hear me as I pray. and
Two to bear my soul away.

Mrs. W. E. Pierce, Town Clerk of Northam, a part of Shrewsbury, Vermont, sang this song handed down through her father, J. K. Spaulding, born in 1837, who was postmaster at West Bridgewater for forty years.

H. H. F., Collector
July 14, 1932

THE HALF-HITCH
(Child 31)

A noble lord in Plymouth did dwell.
He had a fine daughter, a beautiful gal.
A young man of fortune, and riches supplied,
He courted this fair maid to make her his bride,
    To make her his bride,
He courted this fair maid to make her his bride.

He courted her long and he gained her love.
At length this fair maiden intend him to prove.
From the time that she owned him, she fairly denied,

She told him right off, she'd not be his bride,
  She'd not be his bride,
She told him right off she'd not be his bride.

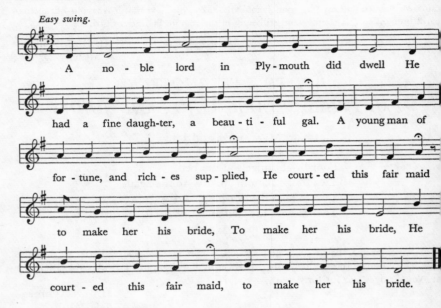

Easy swing.

A no-ble lord in Ply-mouth did dwell He had a fine daugh-ter, a beau-ti-ful gal. A young man of for-tune, and rich-es sup-plied, He court-ed this fair maid to make her his bride, To make her his bride, He court-ed this fair maid, to make her his bride.

Then he said, "Straight home I will steer,"
And many an oath under her he did swear.
He swore he would wed the first woman he see
If she was as mean as a beggar could be,
    As a beggar could be,
If she was as mean as a beggar could be.

She ordered her servants this man to delay.
Her rings and her jewels she soon laid away.
She dressed herself in the worst rags she could find.
She looked like the divil before and behind. Etc.

She clapped her hands on the chimney back,
She crocked her face all over so black,

Then down to the road she flew like a witch
With her petticoat hi-sted upon her half-hitch. Etc.

Soon this young man came riding along.
She stumbled before him, she scarcely could stand
With her old shoes on her feet all tread of askew.
He soon overtook her and said, "Who be you?" Etc.

SPOKEN: "I'm a woman, I s'pose."

This answer grieved him much to the heart.
He wished from his very life he might part.
Then he wished that he had been buried
And then he did ask her and if she was married. Etc.

SPOKEN: "No, I ain't."

This answer suited him much like the rest.
It lay very heavy and hard on his breast.
He found by his oath he must make her his bride.
Then he did ask her behind him to ride. Etc.

SPOKEN: "Your horse will throw me, I know he will."

"O no, O no, my horse he will not,"
So on behind him a-straddle she got.
His heart it did fail him. He dare not go home
For his parents would say, "I'm surely undone." Etc.

So to a neighbor with whom he was great
The truth of the story he dared to relate.
He said, "Here with my neighbor you may tarry
And in a few days with you I will marry." Etc.

SPOKEN: "You won't. I know you won't."

He vowed that he would and straight home he did go.
He acquainted his father and mother also

Of what had befallen him. Now he had sworn.
His parents said to him, "For that don't you mourn. Etc.

"Don't break your vows but bring home your girl
And we'll fix her up and she'll do very well."
The day was appointed. They invited the guests
And then they intended the bride for to dress. Etc.

SPOKEN: "Be married in my old clothes, I s'pose!" Etc.

Married they were and sat down to eat.
With her hands she clawed out the cabbage and meat.
The pudding it burned her fingers so bad
She licked 'em, she wiped 'em along on her rags. Etc.

Hotter than ever, she at it again.
Soon they did laugh til their sides were in pain:
Soon they did say, "My jewel, my bride,
Come sit yourself down by your true lover's side." Etc.

SPOKEN: "Sit in the corner, s'pose, where I used ter."

Some were glad and very much pleased.
Others were sorry and very much grieved.
They ask them to bed the truth to decide
And then they invited both bridegroom and bride. Etc.

SPOKEN: "Give me a light and I'll go alone."

They gave her a light—what could she want more—
And showed her the way up to the chamber door.

SPOKEN: "Husband when you hear my old shoe go
'klonk' then you may come."

Up in the chamber she went klonking about.
His parents said to him, "What think she's about?"
"O mother, O mother, say not one word.
Not one bit of comfort to me this world can afford."

At length they heard her old shoe go klonk.
They gave him a light and bade him go along.
"I choose to go in the dark," he said,
"For I very well know the way to my bed."

He jumped into bed, his back to his bride.
She rolled and she tumbled from side unto side.
She rolled and she tumbled. The bed it did squeak.
He said unto her, "Why can't you lie still?" Etc.

SPOKEN: "I want a light to unpin my clothes."

He ordered a light her clothes to unpin.
Behold she was dressed in the finest of things.
When he turned over her face to behold,
It was fairer to him than silver or gold. Etc.

Up they got and the frolic they had,
For many a heart was merry and glad.
They looked like two flowers just springing from bloom,
With many fair lassies who wished them much joy.

As sung by Mr. James Shepard of Baltimore, Vermont.

H. H. F. and Phillips Barry, Collectors
July 8, 1933

JIMMIE RENDAL
(Child 12)

"Where have you been, Jimmie Rendal, my son,
Where have you been, my own lov-ed one?"
"I've been to see pretty Polly—mother, make my bed soon,
For I'm sick to my heart and I can't but lie down,

Down, derry-down,
Down, derry-down.

For I'm sick to my heart and I can't but lie down."

"What had you for breakfast, Jimmie Rendal, my son,
What had you for breakfast, my own lov-ed one?"
"I had eels fried in butter—mother, make my bed soon,
For I'm sick to my heart and I can't but lie down,

> Down, derry-down,
> Down, derry-down,

For I'm sick to my heart and I can't but lie down."

"What color were they, Jimmie Rendal, my son,
What color were they, my own lov-ed one?"
"They were green, white and checkered—mother, make my bed soon,
For I'm sick to my heart and I can't but lie down.

> Down, derry-down,
> Down, derry-down,

For I'm sick to my heart and I can't but lie down."

"What for your mother, Jimmie Rendal, my son,
What for your mother, my own lov-ed one?"
"My gold and my silver—mother, make my bed soon,
For I'm sick to my heart and I can't but lie down.

> Down, derry-down,
> Down, derry-down,

For I'm sick to my heart and I can't but lie down."

"What for your sister, Jimmie Rendal, my son,
What for your sister, my own lov-ed one?"
"My coach and six horses—mother, make my bed soon,
For I'm sick to my heart and I can't but lie down.

> Down, derry-down,
> Down, derry-down,

For I'm sick to my heart and I can't but lie down."

"What for your brother, Jimmie Rendal, my son,
What for your brother, my own lov-ed one?"
"My gun-shot and powder—mother, make my bed soon,
For I'm sick to my heart and I can't but lie down.

> Down, derry-down,
> Down, derry-down.

For I'm sick to my heart and I can't but lie down."

"What for pretty Polly, Jimmie Rendal, my son,
What for pretty Polly, my own lov-ed one?"
"The gates of Hell wide—mother, make my bed soon,
For I'm sick to my heart and I can't but lie down.

> Down, derry-down,
> Down, derry-down.

For I'm sick to my heart and I can't but lie down."

As sung by Mr. James Shepard, whose songs were learned many years ago in Ireland.
Mr. Shepard lived at Baltimore, Vermont.

H. H. F., Collector
October 29, 1933

BLACK WATER SIDE

On a bright summer's morning as I went a-walking
Viewing the streams that gently did flow,
As the bright sun arose, the hills did adorn
Surrounding the banks of the Black Water Side.
Says he, "My dearest jewel, it's long we have courted,
We're both fit for marriage, I solemnly vow,
And if you're inclined in wedlock to join,
Either 'Yes' or 'No' you must answer me now."

She says, "I'm oppressed and quite in distress.
I'm quite unprepared to answer you now.
My fortune is low, as you very well know,
And to be your bride, you know I'm not fit.

I had some friends went to America
And with my old mother, I mean to reside.
I'll here take my lot in this low little cot
On the lovely sweet banks of the Black Water Side."

Waltz tempo.

On a bright sum-mer's morn-ing As I went a-walk-ing View-ing the streams that gent-ly did flow As the bright sun a-rose the hills did a-dorn sur-round-ing the banks of the Black-wa-ter side Says he my dear-est jew-el, it's long we have court-ed, We're both fit for mar-riage I sol-emn-ly vow And if your in-clined in wed-lock to join me Eith-er "Yes" or "No" you must an-swer me now.

"Well, if you do, you may happen to rue.
I've another in view that won't me deny.
To labor in vain, I'll not ask again.
I'm not set on coaxing, as you may rely.

I gave you the proffer. Accept as the offer
In wee bans of wedlock, we soon would be tied.
You know I adore you and praise none before you,
You blooming sweet maid of the Black Water Side.

"At the age of sixteen, if she's handsome and clean—
As for her fortune, I'm sure I don't care;
As for her clothing, it never will grieve me.
With you I'd range this world so wide.
You're the maid I admire, so grant my desire,
It's you I require from the Black Water Side."

This maid she arose. To her mother she goes
Telling the story as plain as you see.
She got her consent and away they both went.
They were joined in Wedlock's sweet unity.
Their health did increase and troubles grew less.
In peace and in happiness they both do reside.
The truth I am telling. You will find their dwelling
On the lovely sweet banks of the Black Water Side.

. . The old gentleman sings two verses not usually found with "The Bailiff's
Daughter of Islington": *

"O, didn't you know my lily-white hand,
   Likewise my auburn hair;
O, didn't you know that ring of gold
   You gave me once to wear?"

"Right well I know your lily-white hand,
   Right well, your auburn hair,
Right well I know that ring of gold
   That I gave you once to wear."

He looks away. There is his apple orchard across the road. There are walls he

* Published in *Country Songs From Vermont*, p. 36.

laid, meadows flowing luxuriantly down sloping hillsides. There is his tethered calf and there, too, is the Bailiff's Daughter in the aura of:

> "Welcome, luck, and farewell, grief,
> Ten thousand times, to me!
> Thank God, I've caught my own true love
> Who I thought I never would see."

The ballad collector looks far away to a blue line of New Hampshire hills and thinks, "intrusion of 'Lord Bakeman' lines," "half-pitches in a haunting melody," and *this* is the Irish version of the ballad."

Within a few miles she comes upon the riddles sung when Captain Wedderburn, of medieval times, tried expeditiously to win a lady. The ballad is copied from the notebook of Mrs. Margaret A. Martin of Plainfield, New Hampshire as sung by her grandfather, Edward Walsh of Graigue, County Cork, Ireland. It is entitled "A Strange Proposal," and is still redolent of remote period where guessing riddles saved one in the Devil's Courtship and were used "to make mery glee" when Edmund Spenser wrote the elegy for Sidney.

Enigmas were common in very old dialogue-songs. There is the "False False Knight on the Road" (dare I tell that he was the "Devil"—not mentioned in the song because superstition had it that by naming him you summoned the Devil?). When he accosts the little child he asks questions which if answered incorrectly, permit him to make off with the little soul.

The welcome turn of the "King John and the Bishop"* hangs upon right answers to the "King's Three Questions." We are told by Taine of a dialogue between the son of Charlemagne and Alcuin. Alcuin instructs with enigma "in the spirit of the skalds such as we find in the old manuscripts with the barbarian songs." May I add: such as we find *in their tunes*, from barbarian times to this day, in New England.

To revert to King John and the Bishop, it was translated from the Saxon in 1483, but much earlier, this story was sung in northern France. It may have been brought to England with the Conqueror.

Disguises, too, figure in the old songs. They are now as beloved an artifice as when first imagined in creating the old gestes—the tales of adventure

---

* *Garland of Green Mountain Song*, p. 64.

Handed down from early settlers of Gott Island, Maine, we have a fragment of "Hind Horn" seemingly a relique of the Danish Geste of 1,550 verses. Because of his disguise, Hind Horn reveals himself to his love by means of his half of the broken ring. Was this theme ancient when, around 412 B.C., Euripides makes Helen lament: "Were my husband still alive, we might have recognized each other, by having recourse to tokens which ourselves alone would know." Or does it possibly date from 456 A.D. when Childéric, father of Clovis, took refuge in Thuringia, leaving half of a precious ring with a faithful follower who said, according to Gregoire de Tours, "Quand je vous rendrai cette moitié vous pourrez revenir en toute sûreté?" † . . .

Copied from the notebook of Mrs. Margaret A. Martin of Plainfield, New Hampshire, as sung by her grandfather, Edward Walsh of Graigue, County Cork, Ireland. Copied iteratim et punctatim. ("Captain Wedderburn's Courtship")

H. H. F., Collector
November, 1939

A STRANGE PROPOSAL

(Child 46)

> There was a farmer's daughter
> Walking down a narrow lane.
> She met with Mr. Woodburn,
> The keeper of the game.
> He said unto his servant man,
> "Were it not for the law,
> I'd have that maid in bed with me,
> And she lie next the wall."

---

† A Mérouée succéda, en 456, sons fils Childéric. Les Francs, que ce prince irrita par sa luxure, le chassèrent et prirent à sa place, comme chef, le général romain Aegidius. Childéric se refugia dans la Thuringe, laissant dans son pays un Franc qui lui était attaché, pour qu'il apaisât par de douces paroles les esprits furieux. Il lui donna un signe afin que cet homme pût lui faire connaître quand il serait temps de retourner dans sa patrie: ils divisèrent en deux une pièce d'or; Childéric en emporta une moitié, et son ami garda l'autre, disant: "Quand je vous rendrai cette moitié, vous pourrez revenir en toute sûreté." Aegidius était dans la huitième année de son régne, lorsque le fidele ami du roi envoya à son prince des messagers pour lui remettre la moitié de la pièce d'or. Reconnaissant à cet indice que les Francs désiraient son retour, Childéric quitta la Thuringe et fût rétabli dans son pouvoir.

"Go your way, young man," said she,
"And do not trouble me;
Before I would lie one night with you
You must get me dishes three.
Three dishes you must get for me
When I set forth them all
Before I would lie one night with you
And either stock or wall.

"For my breakfast you must get
A cherry without a stone
And for my supper you must get for me
A bird without a bone,
And for my supper you must get for me,
A bird without a gall
Before I would lie one night with you
At either stock or wall."

"When the cherry is in blossom
It really has no stone,
And when the bird is in the egg
I'm sure it has no bone.
The dove it is a gentle bird.
It flies without a gall;
So you and I in one bed will lie
And you'll lie next the wall."

"Go your way, young man," she said,
"And do not me perplex
Before I would lie one night with you
You must answer questions six,
Six questions you must answer me
Where I set forth them all,
Before I would lie one night with you
At either stock or wall."

"What's rounder than a ring,
What's higher than a tree,
What's worse than womankind
And what's deeper than the sea?
What bird sings best; what tree buds first
And where does the dew first fall?
Before I would lie one night with you
At either stock or wall."

"The earth is rounder than a ring;
The sky is higher than a tree;
The Devil is worse than womankind,
And Hell is deeper than the sea.
The thrush sings best, the heath buds first
And on it the dew first falls
And so you and I in one bed will lie
And you'll lie next the wall."

"You must get from me some winter fruit
That in September grew.
You must get for me a mantle
That never wet went through;
A sparrow's horn, a priest unborn,
To join us one and all
Before I'll lie one night with you
At either stock or wall."

"Winter fruits are easily got—
I'll pick for you some haws;
My mother had a mantle,
That never wet went through.
A sparrow's horn is easily got.
There's one in every claw.
Melch isedec was a priest unborn
To join us one and all,
And so you and I in one bed will lie,
And you'll lie next the wall."

Now to conclude and finish
I mean to end my theme.
This couple they got married
And happy do remain.
This young man was so clever
That he did her heart enthrall.
He took her in his arms
And rolled her from the wall.

Mrs. E. M. Sullivan of Springfield, Vermont, sang this as learned in her childhood
Ireland.

H. H. F., Collect
September 21, 19

THE FALSE KNIGHT ON THE ROAD

(Child 3)

"O where are you going?"
Said the false, false knight to the child on the road.
"I'm going to my school,"
Said the pretty boy seven years old.

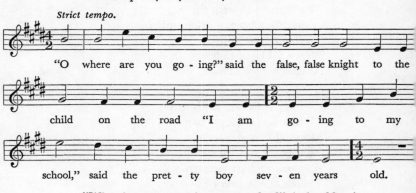

Strict tempo.

"O where are you go-ing?" said the false, false knight to the
child on the road "I am go-ing to my
school," said the pret-ty boy sev-en years old.

"What have you got in your woolen?" (school bag)
Said the false, false knight to the child on the road,
"My books and my dinner,"
Said the pretty boy seven years old.

"Who owns all those cows on the hill?" etc.
"Me and my mamma," etc.

"How many of them are mine?" etc.
"As many as have no tail," etc.

"Who taught you so well?" etc.
"My teachers and my mamma," etc.

"What did they teach you so well for?" etc.
"To keep me from you and from your wicked Hell,"
And he bowed seven times on the road.

"Bad luck to your teacher that taught you so well,"
Said the false, false knight to the child on the road.
"Good luck to the teacher that kept me from you
And from your wicked Hell,"
Said the pretty boy seven years old.

s sung by Mrs. Harriet Gott Murphy of Rumford Centre, Maine. Mrs. Murphy remem-
ers hearing this ballad sung when a small child by her father and uncle, whose ancestors
ere the settlers of Gott Island.

M. O., Collector
September 12, 1942

HIND HORN

(Child 17)

The maid came tripping down the stairs,
Rings on her fingers and gold in her hair,
With a glass of wine all into her hands.
She gave it to the poor old beggarman.

Out of a tumbler he drank the wine;
Into the tumbler he slipped the ring.
She said, "Where did you get this by sea or by land,
Where did you get it—off the drowned man's hand?"

"I neither got it by sea or by land,
Neither did I get it from a drowned man's hand;
My ma-ma gave it to me on her courting day
And I'll give it back on her wedding day."

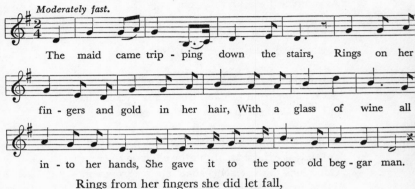

Moderately fast.

The maid came trip-ping down the stairs, Rings on her
fin-gers and gold in her hair, With a glass of wine all
in-to her hands, She gave it to the poor old beg-gar man.

Rings from her fingers she did let fall,
Gold from her hair she did tear off,
Saying, "I'll go with thee forever, ever more,
If I have to beg my bread from door to door."

. . . As many nations as invaded the British Isles have set their mark upon
balladry. The ancient songs were, so to speak, the people's Odyssey, the
Beowulf, their Decameron. Always when people were migrating, there was
interchange of themes in folk tales. As a language penetrated a territory, so c
legends, superstitions, and traditions which were commonly recited or sur

No one knows when the theme of "The Farmer's Curst Wife" enter
British tradition from the Oriental. Mr. Elmer Barton, who grew up in nor
ern Vermont, sings all its lively verses.

Now and then an obvious parallel of ideas recurs as in this quotation fr
the "Satyricon" by Petronius Arbiter: "Being more out of danger amo
the thickets, we cast about where we should hide the gold, that we might
be either charged with the felony, or robbed of it ourselves: at last we cc
cluded to sew it in the lining of an old patched coat." This same effort to hi
gold pieces by sewing them into the lining of a coat reappears, not in Nev
court but in England, in the ballad of "The Yorkshire Boy," Mr. Asa Da
learned from his Irish grandfather a finely humorous version.

Less hypothetical as to origin is "Lord Bakeman" in that it follows closely tale in manuscript, early 1300, seemingly about the father of Thomas á cket.

Anglo-Saxon ballads often hark back to remote paganism. There is the loved "John Barleycorn"* which even now is taken seriously by some asants for seedtime and harvest—their rites to ensure a fine crop the coming ar in the death and rebirth of the corn. . . .

sung by Mr. Elmer Barton of Quechee, Vermont. Learned when a young boy from uncle who lived in the northern part of the state.

M. Olney, Collector
August 13, 1945

FARMER'S CURST WIFE

(Child 278)

There was an old man who bought him a farm
    Saying low-land tick-le O lay.
There was an old man who bought him a farm
And he had no team to carry it on
    Saying low-land tick-le O laddie,
    Low-land tick-le O lay.

(*Follow pattern of the first verse for remaining verses*)

So he yoked up his dog beside his sow
He yoked up his dog beside his sow
And he went walloping 'round, the Devil knows how

But he met the old Devil on one certain day.
He met the old Devil on one certain day
Saying: "One of your family I'll carry away."

"O," out cries the old man, "I am undone!"
Out cries the old man, "I am undone!
The Devil has come for my oldest son!"

---

* *Country Songs of Vermont*, p. 2.

"No, it is not your son," the Devil did say,
" 'Tis not your son, the Devil did say
But your scolding old wife—I'll carry away."

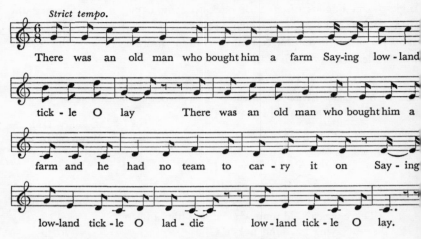

Strict tempo.

There was an old man who bought him a farm Say-ing low-land
tick - le O lay   There was an old man who bought him a
farm and he had no team to car - ry it on Say - ing
low-land tick - le O lad - die   low - land tick - le O lay.

"O take her, O take her with all my heart!
Take her, O take her with all my heart
And I hope and pray you will never part!"

So the old Devil swung her across his back
The old Devil swung her across his back
And up to Hell's door he went clickerty-clack.

There was one little Devil preparing the chains,
There was one little Devil preparing the chains,
While she up with her foot and she kicked out his brains.

Then another little Devil said, "Hitch her up higher!"
Another little Devil said, "Hitch her up higher!"
For she up with her foot and she kicked nine in the fire.

Then another little Devil peeked over the wall,
Another little Devil peeked over the wall;
"Carry her back, master Devil, she will kill us all!"

So the old Devil he swung her across his back,
The old Devil he swung her across his back
And like a darn fool he went tugging her back.

And the old Devil he throwed her down on the floor,
The old Devil he throwed her down on the floor
Saying, "Got to stay here—go to Hell no more!"

Then out cried the old man, "You were born for a curse!"
Out cried the old man, "You were born for a curse
You've been to Hell now you're a whole lot worse!"

ung by Mr. Asa Davis of Milton, Vermont, as learned from his father.

H. H. F., Collector
November 8, 1945

THE YORKSHIRE BOY

(Child 283)

In London there lived a mason by trade.
He had him two servants, a man and a maid.
The Yorkshire boy, he had for his man,
And to do his business, his name it was John.

Timi fol dol di lie do fol lol der day.

'Twas early one morning he called his man John.
John hearing his master unto him did run,
Says, "Take this cow and drive her to the fair,
For she is cross and she hooked my old mare."

CHORUS:

John he took the cow all out of the barn,
And drove her to the fair, as we do learn,

And then pretty soon, he met some men
And sold them the cow for six pounds, ten.

(Repeat chorus after each verse)

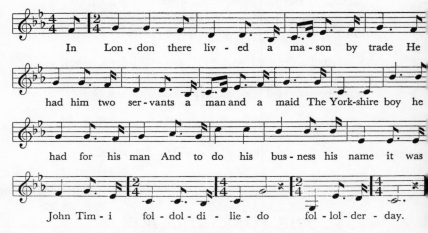

In Lon-don there liv-ed a ma-son by trade He
had him two ser-vants a man and a maid The York-shire boy he
had for his man And to do his bus-ness his name it was
John Tim-i fol-dol-di-lie-do fol-lol-der-day.

He went to the tavern to get him some drink,
For the good old farmers paid him down the chink.
He went to the landlady and thus he did say,
"Oh, what shall I do with my money, I pray."

"All in your coat lining I'll sew it up," she said,
"For fear that on the highway robbed you may be."
The highwayman sat behind a drinking of wine,
And he said to himself, "That money is all mine."

John took his leave and away he did go.
The highwayman followed after him also.
He overtook the boy well on the highway,
"You're well overtaken young man," he did say.

They went till they came to the long, dark lane.
The highwayman said to the boy, "I'll tell you all plain.

Deliver up your money without fear or strife
Or here in this place I will end your sweet life."

John seeing no room for any dispute,
Put his hand in his coat lining and pulled the money out,
Out of his coat lining he pulled the money out,
And in the tall grass he strew it all about.

The highwayman getting down from his horse,
But little did he think it was for his loss.
While he was picking money up that was strewed,
John mounted on his horse and away he rode.

The highwayman followed after him for to stay.
John minded nothing about him, but still rode away.
Home to his master, he did bring
Horse, saddle and bridle and many things.

The maid saw the boy as he was returning home,
And for to tell his master went in the other room.
The old man came to the door and he said, "What a fox,
Has my old cow turned into a hoss?"

"Oh, no, my good master, your cow I have sold,
Being robbed on the highway by the highwayman bold.
While he was picking money up that I strewed,
I mounted on his horse and away I rode."

The saddle bags being opened as I've been told,
Five hundred pounds of silver and gold,
Besides a pair of pistols. Says John says he, "I vow,
I think, my good old master, I've well sold your cow."

"I think for a boy you have done very rare,
Three quarters of this money you shall have for your share
And as for the old villain you have served him just right,
For you have put upon him the sure Yorkshire Bite."

Sung by Asa Davis of Milton, Vermont, as learned from his grandfather, Charles Atkins
of Duxbury, Vermont.

H. H. F., Collector
June 23, 1939

LORD BAKEMAN

(Child 53)

In India lived a noble lord,
Whose riches were beyond compare;
He was the darling of his parents,
And of his estate the only heir.

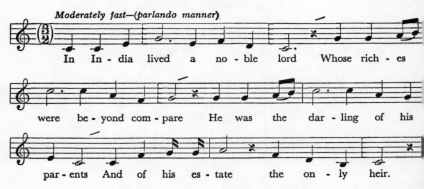

Oh, he had gold and he had silver,
And he had houses of high degree,
But he could never be contented,
Until a voyage he had been to sea.

He sail-ed east, he sail-ed west,
Until he came to the Turkish shore.
There he was taken and put in prison,
Where he could neither see nor hear.

For seven long months he lay lamenting,
He lay lamenting in iron chains.
There happened to be a brisk young lady,
Who released him out of his iron bands.

The jailer had an only daughter,
And a brisk young lady gay was she.
As she was a-walking across the floor,
She chanced Lord Bakeman to see.

She stole the keys of her father's prison,
And vowed Lord Bakeman she would set free.
She went into the prison door,
And opened it without delay.

"Have you got gold, have you got silver?
And have you houses of high degree?
What will you give to the lady fair,
If she from bondage will set you free?"

"Yes, I've got gold and I've got silver,
And I have houses of high degree
And I'll give them all to the lady fair,
If she from bondage will set me free."

"I do not want your gold nor silver,
Nor your houses of high degree.
All I want for is to make me happy,
And all I crave is your fair bodee."

"Let us make a bargain and make it strong,
For seven long years it shall stand:
You shall not marry no other woman,
Nor I'll not marry no other man."

The seven long years had gone and passed.
The seven long years were at an end.
She pack-ed up all her rich gay clothing,
Saying: "Now I'll go and seek a friend."

She sail-ed east, she sail-ed west,
Until she came to the Indian shore.
There she could never be contented
Till for Lord Bakeman she did inquire.

She inquired for Lord Bakeman's palace
At every corner of the street.
She did inquire for Lord Bakeman's palace,
Of every person she chanced to meet.

And when she came to Lord Bakeman's palace,
She knocked so loud upon the ring,
There was no one so ready as the brisk young porter
To arise and let this fair lady in.

"Oh, is this Lord Bakeman's palace?
And is the Lord himself within?"
"Oh, yes, oh, yes," cries the brisk young porter.
"He and his new bride have just entered in."

She wept, she wept, she wrung her hands,
Crying, "Alas, I am undone.
I wish I was in my native country,
Across the seas there to remain.

"Tell him to send me an ounce of bread,
And a bottle of his wine so strong,
And ask him if he has forgot the lady
Who released him out of his iron bands."

The porter went unto his master,
He knelt so low upon one knee.
"Arise, arise, my brisk young porter,
And tell to me what the matter is."

"There is a lady stands at your gate.
And she doth weep most bitterly.
I think she is the finest creature,
That ever I chanced my eyes to see.

"She's got more rings on her four fingers,
And around her waist a diamond band;
She's got more gold about her clothing,
Than your bride and all her kin.

"She wants you to send her an ounce of bread,
And a bottle of your wine so strong,
And ask you if you have forgot the lady
Who released you out of your iron bands?"

He jumped into the middle of the floor,
He smashed the table in pieces three,
"You came here on a horse and saddle,
You may ride home in a coach and three."

Then up spoke his new bride's mother,
And she was a lady of high degree,
" 'Tis you have married my only daughter,
Why, she is none the worse for thee."

"But since my fair one has arrived,
A second wedding there shall be.
Your daughter came on a horse and saddle,
She may ride home in a coach and three."

He took his fair lady by the hand;
He led her over the marble stone.
He changed her name from Susannah Fayer
To be the wife of Lord Bakeman.

He took her by the lily-white hand,
He led her through from room to room,
He changed her name from Susannah Freeman
To be the wife of Lord Bakeman.

He took her by the lily-white hand,
He led her across the marble stone,
He changed her name from Susannah Freeman
To be the wife of Lord Bakeman.

. There is also the wren, which in Egyptian lore was "the king of all birds."
is little fellow, on St. Stephen's Day, is captured when all the people turn
t for the "beating of the bush." A singer from County Cork, Ireland, told

us, "Men, women, and children come out to hunt the wren. It lives in th
walls which are made of mud, back of which is a kind of fir tree which cann
grow here (in the United States). After capturing the wren, they attach it
a high stick and carry it through the village singing this song. They never g
to bed without seeing that the broom is behind the door—to keep the faeri
out." Scholars consider this song a direct descendant of Druidism.

Does the precaution about the broom behind the door relate to tradition
notions of pre-Christian times when the Greeks and northern Druids adopte
religious beliefs from the older Egyptians? Broom is also called "besom
Bonwick, writing in "Irish Druids and Irish Religions" states: "The bars
or bundle of twigs is held by the Parsee priests." Further on he tells (page 11
"they divined . . . by the croaking of their ravens and chirping of tame wrens

Another authority, the Senchus Mor,* translated by Hancock an
O'Mahoney, may show Druid intrusions into Christian-Irish beliefs. Bonwi
adds: "Some of the ideas developed in that Christian work were suppose
traditional notions of earlier and Druicidal times." . . .

Text written down by Mrs. Harry Thomas, as sung by her mother, Mrs. E. M. Sulliv
of Springfield, Vermont.

H. H. F., Collect
March 1, 1940

THE WRAN

The wran, the wran, the king of all birds,
Saint Stephen's Day, he was caught in the firs;
Drolin, drolin, where is your nest?
It's in a place that I love best.

Between the holly and ivy tree
Were all the birds come singing to me,
Sing holly, sing ivy,
To keep next Christmas, it will be holly.

On Christmas day I turned the spit.
I burned my finger, I feel it yet.

---

* One of the earliest and most important portions of the ancient laws of Ireland.

Between my finger and my thumb
There lies a big blister as big as a plum.

As I was going up Straw Hall
I met a wran upon the wall;
Up with my stick and I gave him a fall,
And I brought him here to visit you all.

Behind the door, the broom it stands,
Which causes my mistress a greasy floor;
Up with the kettle and down with the pot,
Give us our answer and let us be gone.

If you will fill it with the small, (small beer)
It will not answer my boys at all;
But if you fill it up of the best,
I hope it's in heaven your soul may rest.

. . Certain songs, still currently known, seem to antedate the Norman Con-
quest. "Sir Lionel" in a magical wood kills a wild boar. By the time it is
handed down in the family of Dr. Albert Ferguson and recorded in Middlebury, Vermont, the boar has become a wild bear—all in a fine tune. (It is a
tune you cannot shake, once heard.)

Another ballad is set in a medieval forest, with a memorable story. "The
Burly, Burly Banks of Barbry-O" is of ancient lineage even though there is
the anachronism of a penknife, an addition of later generations.

We can step from medieval wood to medieval wood, from penknife to penknife, if we include here "The Cruel Mother," as sung in Houlton, Maine, by
Mrs. W. H. Smith. . . .

As sung by Dr. Alfred Ferguson of Middlebury, Vermont. This version was learned fro
his mother whose ancestors came from Massachusetts.

M. Olney, Collect
July 14, 1942

OLD BANGUM
(Child 18)

Old Bangum would a-hunting ride,
Derrum, derrum, derrum.
Old Bangum would a-hunting ride,
Kili-ko
Old Bangum would a-hunting ride
With sword and pistol by his side.
Derrum-kili-ko-ko.

(*Above pattern used for all verses.*)

He rode unto the riverside.
Where he a pretty maid espied.

"Fair maid," said he, "will you marry me?"
"Ah no," said she, "for we'd ne'er agree."

"There lives a bear in yonder wood,
He'd eat your bones, he'd drink your blood."

Brave Bangum rode to the wild bear's den,
Where lay the bones of a thousand men.

Brave Bangum and the wild bear fought;
At set of sun the bear was naught.

He rode again to the riverside
To ask that maid to be his bride.

ing by Mr. Elmer Barton of Quechee, Vermont.

M. Olney, Collector
1942

THE BURLY, BURLY BANKS OF BARBRY-O
(Child 14)

There were three sisters picking flowers
High in the lea and the lonely O.
They scarce had picked but one or two,
On the burly, burly banks of Barbry-O.

It's there they spied a bank-robber bold.
It's there they spied a bank-robber bold.

He took the oldest by the hand.
He hurled her round 'n he made her stand,

Saying, "Will you be a bank-robber's wife?
Or will you die by my penknife?"

"No, I won't be a bank-robber's wife;
I'd rather die by your penknife."

Then he took out his penknife;
It's there he ended her sweet life.

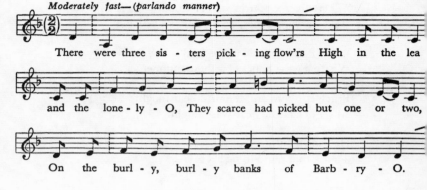

There were three sis - ters pick - ing flow'rs High in the lea
and the lone - ly - O, They scarce had picked but one or two,
On the burl - y, burl - y banks of Barb - ry - O.

(Follow pattern for burden in the following verses)

He took the next one by the hand.
He hurled her round; he made her stand,

Saying, "Will you be a bank-robber's wife?
Or will you die by my penknife?"

"No, I won't be a bank-robber's wife;
I'd rather die by your penknife."

Then he took out his penknife
And it's there he ended her sweet life.

He took the youngest by the hand,
He hurled her round; he made her stand,

Saying, "Will you be a bank-robber's wife?
Or will you die by my penknife?"

"Yes, I will be a bank-robber's wife
So I won't die by your penknife.

"O dear, O dear, I wish my two brothers were here!"
"O what would your two brothers do?"

"For one is a minister; the other like you
On the burly, burly banks of Barbry-O."

Then he took out his penknife,
And it's there he ended his own life.

. . . Another ballad dealing with the supernatural is "The Wife of Usher's
Well"—an Irish version as sung by Mrs. Phyllis MacDonald Burditt of Springfield, Vermont. Not supernatural, but vividly natural, are the sons who, though
dead, return to the mother who can revel in doing for them as of old.

After the Norman invasion, downtrodden Saxons were fascinated that one
man, in Lincoln Forest, had the temerity to live his own life (off the rich),
express his own creed (give to the poor) and choose his own form of recrea-
tion (hunting, archery, disguises, etc.). Tales of Robin Hood delighted them,
in his plays of wit, in his caprices with would-be captors, and fellowship with
his "merry men all."

Needless to say, we always have "an ear to the ground" for a Robin Hood
ballad. Up near the "Canady Line" in New Hampshire, Miss Olney recorded
"Bold Robin Hood and the Pedlar."

In the region of Mt. Katahdin, in Maine, we heard:

"Five hundred and ten of bold Robin Hood's men
Came trippeling over the hill."

Baffled silence . . . "All I can remember."

"Who sang it to you?" A chance address led us several miles north. There
we found entire the ballad of "Robin Hood Rescuing the Three Squires."

Robin Hood ballads were in circulation some time before William Langland, in "Piers Plowman," mentioned them in 1377. Sleuthe says:

"I can nouzte perfitly my pater-noster as the prest it syngeth,
But I can rymes of Robyn Hood and Randolf erle of Chestre."

This is taken from the B-text as published by Oxford (1886) at the Clarendon
Press, edited from numerous manuscripts by the Rev. Walter William Skeat,
Litt. D., Ll. D. Just short of a hundred years later, in 1473, John Paston
writes of a servant who has been kept "Thys iij yer to pleye Seynt Jorge and
Robyn Hod and the shryff of Nottingham," showing the ballads were more

than sung by that time; they were enacted. Our Maine singer was a section hand on the Bangor and Aroostook Railroad. He and William Langland and John Paston had never been introduced. It didn't matter. They knew their ballads.

A sense of chronology leads me to cite here, "Sir Andrew Bardeen, a found in Staceyville, Maine, in 1940. Several of the river drivers on the . .

Sung by Mrs. Phyllis Burditt of Springfield, Vermont.

M. Olney, Collecto
October 11, 1951

THE WIFE OF USHER'S WELL
(Child 79)

There lived a wife at Usher's Well
And a wealthy wife was she;
She had three stout and stalwart sons
And sent them o'er the sea.
They had not been a week from her,
A week but barely one,
When word came to the carline wife
That her three sons were gone.

They had not been a week from her
A week but barely three,
When word came to the carline wife
That her sons she'd never see.
"I wish the wind may never cease
Nor fishes in the flood,
Till my three sons come home to me
In earthly flesh and blood!"

It fell about the Martinmas,
When nights are long and mirk,
The carline wife's three sons came home
And their hats were on the birk.

There lived a wife at Ush - ers Well And a
wealth - y wife was she. She had three stout and
stal - wart sons And sent them o'er the sea, They
had not been a week from her A week but bare - ly one,
When word came to the car - line wife That her three sons were gone.

It neither grew in syke nor ditch,
Nor yet in any sheugh,
But at the gates of Paradise
That birk grew fair enough.

"Blow up the fires, my maidens fair!
Bring water from the well!
For all my house shall feast this night
Since my three sons are well!"
And she has made for them a bed
She's made it long and wide;
And she's taken her mantle round about,
Sat down at their bedside.

Up then did crow the red, red cock
And up and crew the gray;
The eldest to the youngest said,
" 'Tis time we were away."

The cock he hadent crowed but once
And clapped his wings away
When the youngest to the eldest said,
"O, Brother, we must away!"

The cock doth crow, the day doth dawn,
The channerin worm doth chide;
"Gin we be miss out of our place,
A sair pain we maun bide.
Fare you well, my mother dear!
Farewell to barn and byre!
And fare you well, the bonny lass
That kindles my mother's fire!"

Sung by Mrs. W. H. Smith of Houlton, Maine. Her parents were from Canada.

H. H. F., Collector
September 23, 1940

THE CRUEL MOTHER

(Child 20)

In New York lived a lady fair
All alone and alone-y!
There she had two pretty little babes
Down by the greenwood side-y!

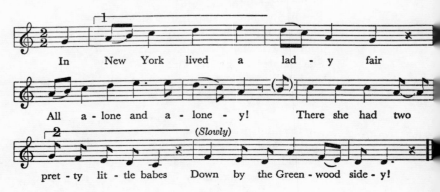

In New York lived a lad-y fair
All a-lone and a-lone-y! There she had two
(Slowly)
pret-ty lit-tle babes Down by the Green-wood side-y!

"O babes, O babes, if you were mine,
All alone and alone-y,
I would dress you up in silks so fine
Down by the greenwood side-y."

"O mother, dear, we once were thine,
All alone and alone-y.
You neither dressed us coarse or fine,
Down by the greenwood side-y.

"But you had a penknife keen and sharp
All alone and alone-y.
You pierced us both to the tender hearts,
Down by the greenwood side-y.

"You dug a hole both wide and deep,
All alone and alone-y
You laid us down and bade us sleep,
Down by the greenwood side-y."

Sung by Mrs. Belle Richards of Colebrook, New Hampshire, as learned from her father,
Mr. Luther, of Pittsburg, New Hampshire, who was born in Canada.

M. Olney, Collector
November 20, 1941

BOLD ROBIN HOOD AND THE PEDLAR

(Child 132)

"What have you got, you pedlar trim?
What have you got, pray tell to me?"
"It's seven suits of the gay green silk,
Beside my bow-strings two or three."

"If you've seven suits of the gay green silk,
Besides your bow-strings two or three;
Upon my word," said Little John,
"One half of them belong to me."

The pedlar then took off his pack,
And laid it down most manfully,
Saying, "The man that can drive me two feet from this,
The pack and all I will give to thee."

Moderately fast.

What have you got you ped - lar trim What
have you got pray tell to me, It's sev - en suits
of the gay green silk Be - side my bow-strings two or three.

Then Little John he drew his sword.
The noble pedlar held his hand.
They swaggered swords till the sweat did drop,
Saying, "Noble pedlar, stay your hand.

Then Robin Hood, he drew his sword.
The noble pedlar held his hand.
They swaggered swords till the blood did drop,
Saying, "Noble pedlar, stay your hand."

"What is your name, you pedlar trim?
What is your name, pray tell to me?"
"Not one bit of it—of my name you'll get
Till both of yours you tell to me."

"My name is Bold Robin Hood,
The other Little John so free,
And now it lies within your breast
To tell us what your name can be."

"My name is Bold Gammon gay,
And I came far beyond the sea;

For killing a man in my father's court
I was banished from my own country."

"Your name it is Bold Gammon gay,
And you came far beyond the sea;
And if we are two sister's sons;
What nearer kindred need we be?"

First recorded on the Sound-Scriber, from the singing of Mr. Charles Fennimore in
Bridgewater, Maine.

H. H. F. and M. Olney, Collectors
September 24, 1942

BOLD ROBIN HOOD RESCUING THE
THREE SQUIRES

(Child 140)

Bold Robin Hood marched along the highway,
Along the highway marched he,
Until he met with a lady fair
A-weeping along the highway.

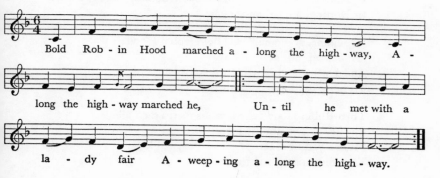

Bold Rob-in Hood marched a-long the high-way, A-
long the high-way marched he, Un-til he met with a
la-dy fair A-weep-ing a-long the high-way.

"O do you mourn for gold," he says,
"Or do you mourn for fee,
Or do you mourn for any high knight
That deserted your company?"

"No, I don't mourn for gold," she said,
"Nor I don't mourn for fee,
Nor I don't mourn for any high knight
That deserted my company.

"But I do mourn for my three sons,
Today they're condemned to die;
In Nottingham town so fast they lie bound,
In Nottingham prison they lie."

"O have they sat any temple on fire
Or any high knight have they slain
Or have they enticed fair maidens to sin
Or with married men's wives have they lain?"

"No, they've not sat any temple on fire
Nor any high knight have they slain
Nor they've not enticed fair maidens to sin
Nor with married men's wives they've not lain.

"But they have killed the King's fallow deer.
Today they're condemned to die.
In Nottingham town so fast they lie bound,
In Nottingham prison they lie."

"Go home, go home," said bold Robin Hood.
"And weep no more to-day
And I will stand hangman this livelong day
To hang the Squires all three."

Then Robin Hood called on his merry men all,
By one, by two and by three.
"When you hear three blasts on my bugle horn
You must hasten most speedily."

Bold Robin Hood marched along the highway.
Along the highway marched he,
Until he met with an old beggarman
A-begging along the highway.

"Good morning, good morning, my old beggarman,
What news do you bring to me?"
"There is weeping and wailing in all Nottingham
For the loss of the Squires all three."

"Come change your clothing," said bold Robin Hood,
"Come change your clothing for mine.
Here's fifty bright guineas I'll give in exchange.
'Twill buy you cake and wine."

Robin Hood put on the beggarman's clothes.
They were made of hemp and tow.
"They will cause me to scrub," said bold Robin Hood,
"But further to-day I must go."

Bold Robin Hood marched along the highway,
Along the highway marched he,
Until he met with the Master High Sheriff,
And with him the Squires three.

"Good morning, good morning, my old beggarman,
What can I do for thee?"
"I want to stand hangman this livelong day
To hang the Squires three."

"Yes you can have all of their gay clothing,
And all of their bright monee,
And you may stand hangman this livelong day,
To hang the Squires three."

"I don't want none of their gay clothing,
Nor none of their bright monee;
But I want three blasts on my bugle horn
That their souls in Heaven might be."

Bold Robin Hood marched to the gallus so high,
To the gallus so high marched he,
And by his side was the Master High Sheriff
And with him the Squires three.

He put the bugle unto his mouth.
He blew it loud and shrill.
A hundred and ten of bold Robin Hood's men
Come trippeling over the hill.

"Whose men, whose men?" cried the High Sheriff,
"Whose men? I pray, tell me."
"They are mine and not thine," said bold Robin Hood,
"Come to borrow three Squires of thee."

"O take them, O take them," then cried the High Sheriff,
"O take them, O take them," cried he;
"But there's not another beggar in all Nottingham
Could borrow three more from me."

Sung by Mr. Hanford Hayes in Staceyville, Maine.

H. H. F., Collecto:
September 22, 194(

ANDREW MARTEEN

(Child 250)

In bon-ey Scotland three brothers did dwell,
Three brothers did dwell, the three,
And all did cast lots to see which of them
Would go robbing down on the salt sea.
And all did cast lots to see which of them
Would go robbing down on the salt sea.

The lots they fell on Andrew, fourteen,
The youngest of those brothers three,
That he should go robbing down on the salt sea
To maintain his two brothers and he.
That he should go robbing down on the salt sea
To maintain his two brothers and he.

As he was a-sailing one fine summer's morning
Just as the day did appear,
He spied a large vessel a-sailing far off
And at last she came sailing quite near.

"Art thou, art thou?" cried Andrew Marteen,
"Art thou, a-sailing so high?"
"A rich merchant-ship from Old England's shores
And please will you let me pass by?"

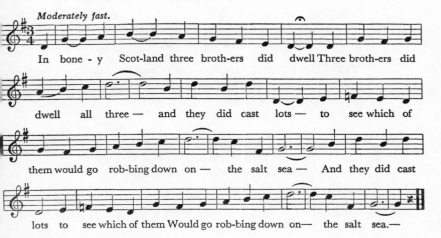

In bone-y Scot-land three broth-ers did dwell Three broth-ers did dwell all three — and they did cast lots — to see which of them would go rob-bing down on — the salt sea — And they did cast lots to see which of them Would go rob-bing down on— the salt sea.—

"O no, O no," cried Andrew Marteen,
"It's a thing that can't very well be;
Your ship and your cargo I will take away,
And you body feed to the salt sea."

The news it went back to Old England's shore.
King Henry he wore the crown.
His ship and his cargo were all cast away
And his mariners they were all drowned.

"Come build me a boat," cried Captain Charles Stewart,
"And build it both safe and secure,
And if I don't bring in that Andrew Marteen,

My life I will never endure.
And if I don't bring in that Andrew Marteen,
My life I will never endure."

As he was a-sailing one fine summer's morning,
Just as the day did appear,
He spied a large vessel a-sailing far off,
And at length it came sailing quite near.

"Art thou, art thou?" cried Captain Charles Stewart,
"Art thou a-sailing so high?"
"A Scotch bone-y robber from Old Scotland's shore,
And it's please will you let me pass by?"

"O no, O no," cried Captain Charles Stewart,
"It's a thing that can't very well be;
Your ship and your cargo I will take away,
And you body feed to the salt sea."

"Fire on, fire on!" cried Andrew Marteen,
"Your talk I don't value one pin.
Your brass at your side makes a very fine show
But I'm pure steel within."

Broadside to broadside those two came together;
Their cannons like thunder did roar.
When Captain Charles Stewart took Andrew, fourteen,
And they hung him on Old England's shore.

. . . East Branch of the Penobscot can sing of the heroic Sir Andrew Bardeen
though they do not know it is about Sir Andrew Barton, a Scottish nava
commander, turned pirate. How would they regard him if they knew furthe
that he is said to have taken great pleasure and pride in sending to his kin
(James the Fourth) three barrels of pickled pirates' heads (in 1506)? Natur
ally he could come to no good end.

From those times also, was sung "The Death of Queen Jane" a loved wif
of King Henry VIII, in the manner of speaking. Lines from that same song
though dealing with "Two Dukes" were handed down as a bedtime song i
a Roxbury, Vermont, home. Not many years later the ballad of "The Fou

[aries," which is these days sung by Mrs. Charles Lansing of Melrose, [assachusetts, may have developed. In Scotland, singers seem to have retold [e tragic death of one of the four Marys who came with Mary Stuart from [rance to Scotland, in 1561.

We have innumerable songs dating from Elizabethan days. How do we [now?' Certain ballads were quoted in snatches, in Beaumont and Fletcher's [The Knight of the Burning Pestle," in 1611. This is true of "King William [nd Sweet Margaret" charmingly sung by Mrs. Winifred Haskins of Savoy, [assachusetts, and by Asa Davis of Milton, Vermont; true also of "Lord [anner" which we have found in northern New England states. The version [f the latter which seems to have the longest family history was furnished as [Lord Arnold" by Mr. George J. Edwards of Burlington, Vermont. When I [rst met Mr. Edwards he told me that his grandfather had always taught the [order ballads to his own family, as history. As one example only of the many [nstances where we record genealogical data for the ballad, I quote from his [tter:

The song has been handed down from one to another in our family for nearly [wo hundred years as follows. My great grandfather, Henry W. Edwards, whose [ife was Margaret Douglas of Scotland, was born in Westchester, England, in [739 and died in 1820, my grandfather, William H. Edwards whose wife was [fartha Bennings, a Northumberland girl, was born in the town of Seaton, in [he East Riding of Yorkshire, England, in 1785 and died on the second day of [uly 1881, the day that President Garfield was shot.

My father, Henry R. Edwards whose wife was an American woman, a native [f Vermont, by the name of Wetherell, was also born in the town of Seaton, in [he East Riding of Yorkshire, England, in 1826 and died in 1895.

This song was passed down from my great grandfather, or grandmother, I do [ot know which, to my grandfather, who in turn taught it to my father, and also [me, as he did many other songs including several of the so-called "border [ngs." This is a record for the song that I think few can equal.

Again, it is a matter of history that the royal court was held at Winchester, in [he county of Hampshire, in the south of England, prior to the year one thousand, [nd was known and referred to as the Hampshire Court. It was, however, re-[oved to Westminster by Edward the Confessor for a comparatively short time [ut was again restored to its former location in Hampshire by King William the [onqueror about 1068 and remained there some time, during the reign of [Ienry I and Henry II.

Referring to the verse that reads as follows, "Lord Arnold has gone to the Hampshire Court King Henry for to see" seems to me better and more appropriate than anything offered in the other versions. The description of the foot page's journey to the court is much more natural and lucid than anything the other selections give. Again, as follows, when Lord Arnold arrived at his castle, "Lord Arnold he summond his merry men all, by one's, by two's and by three's, he ordered them not a drum should be beat, nor a bugle sounded be." What could be more natural, or plainly stated than this? It seems to me the other versions suffer, in comparison with this.

Again, "Lord Arnold strode through the castle halls and opened the door so wide, they did not know that Lord Arnold had come, till he stood by their bedside." Or this, when Mottha Grow answered Lord Arnold's order to arise, "Must I arise, said Mottha Grow, and fight you for my life, while you have a glittering sword by your side and I have not a knife." And Lord Arnold's answer, "Yes I have a sword, here at my side, and others in their place, and you shall have the best one of them and I will take the worst." The other selections give it as two swords by his side. I never knew or heard of a man wearing two swords at one time, did you?

I never heard this piece sung by anybody outside of my own family and was greatly surprised to learn that it was so widely scattered.

November 1, 1933.   /s/ George J. Edwards

Thus we have a family tradition which, authentic history, or no, casts its own illumination on a ballad. Another instance is given regarding the two verses Mr. Edwards remembered of "The Rose of England" from the singing of his grandfather, Mr. William Edwards. He had been told that the Red Rose was Henry VII. Richard was called the "White Boar." He slew the Red Rose and prophesied that the Red Rose would bloom again. The Earl of Granby took the nephew and hid him in Northumberland. Later he took him to Brittany and kept him there until of age. When they returned to England the Earl of Saxon "the Blue Boar" fought Richard "the White Boar" and slew him. Then the Red Rose bloomed again.

In 1937, I was told by the ballad authority, Phillips Barry, of Cambridge Massachusetts, that the "Rose of England"—though in the Percy MS—had never been recovered in oral tradition. Incomplete as this is, it should be appreciated thus. The title of this ballad is quoted in a play by Fletcher in 1639.

Another extremely rare ballad was handed down many generations in

Mr. Edward's family as "The Trooper and the Turk." In the Child Collection a Scottish form is known as "John Thompson and the Turk." The Northumberland version should be unique to scholars in that it ends differently than the Scottish one.

Also from the Douglas branch of his family, Mr. Edwards recalled the 'Edward Ballad." His grandfather always thought the tragedy occurred at Roslin Castle, one of the famous old castles near Edinburgh, Scotland. A genealogy was compiled by Father Hay from genealogical records from the time of William the Conqueror in English and Latin of the St. Clair family. This gives no generation in which there were two brothers, Edward and John.

For comparison, we have the way it was sung in Rhode Island some forty years ago, although learned in Amherst, Massachusetts.

On the Scottish Border there was plenty of incident to be resung as news. James McGill of Lindores in 1679 performed a feat of arms which may have occasioned the ballad of "Johnny Scott." Mr. Jonathan Moses of Orford, New Hampshire, learned it from his father during his childhood in the Adirondack mountains. He learned another ballad, a most gory atrocity, commonly called "False Lamkin." His father knew it as "Squire Relantman."

It is difficult to attribute rightly certain ballads to certain reigns. In the case of "The Blind Beggar of Bethnal Green," Bishop Percy of Percy's "Reliques" can be quoted. He thinks it likely that the song was made up in the reign of Queen Elizabeth "from the arms of England being called 'the Queen's arms' and from its tune being quoted in other old pieces in her time."

The home of the Blind Beggar of Bednal Green was supposed to be Kirby Castle. Samuel Pepys terms it "a very fine place" in his diary, June 25th, 1663.

Our singer learned it as the "Blind Beggar," not of Bethnal Green, but of Bethelhem-town—a name that presumably made more sense to some earlier singer. In fact, like a game of "gossip," words alter in folk-transmission, but they must always make sense to the singer. This can account for occasional New England adaptations of words or locales. In southern New Hampshire, a version of "Lady Isabel and the Elf-Knight" runs:

> "She then did mount her milkwhite steed
> And led the turban gray
> And rode till she came to Boston town
> Two hours before it was day."

In Siberia, a suburb of Staceyville, Maine, a fragment of "King John and the Bishop" ends with

> "You think I'm the Bishop of Canterbury
> But I'm nawthing but his *hired man*."

When Fair Elinor, jilted by her lover, Lord Thomas, breaks down his resistance by appearing at his wedding to the Brown Girl,

> "He took her by her lily-white hand
> And led her across the floor
> And seated her in a *rocking chair*
> Among the ladies there."*

Some day I hope to understand why in the stables of wealthy lords, the folk know that if there are any horses, there are always "thirty and three," why many disasters come under cover of darkness "three hours before it was day." Often an exciting song begins with "As carelessly I strayed." Vivid words are chosen that enhance usual meaning. Here are several: "Clay-cold corpse," "herding *of* their flocks," "Dinner was served *up* soon," "gold in store," "on the shore stood a woman lone and lonely." Contrition comes again and again in songs where criminals say, "My soul is fit for Hell." . .

Mrs. Maude Parks, now living at 1308 36th Street, N. W. Washington, D. C. learned this fragment from her mother, Mrs. Marian Averill, of Roxbury, Vermont.

H. H. F., Collector
February 19, 1948

TWO DUKES

(Child 170)

> As two men were a-walking
> Down by the seaside
> They espied a dead body
> Washed out by the tide.

---

* *Vermont Folk Songs and Ballads*, p. 209.

They took out his bowels;
They stretched forth his feet;
They embalm-ed his body
In spices so sweet.

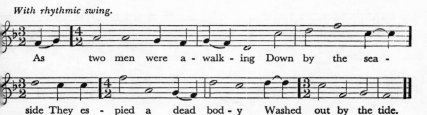

With rhythmic swing.

As two men were a - walk - ing Down by the sea -
side They es - pied a dead bod - y Washed out by the tide.

Six men went before him;
Six bore him to the ground;
Six maidens followed after
In their black velvet gowns.

sung by Mrs. Charles Lansing, of Massachusetts, who says: "I have known this for a
mber of years; seems as though I have always known it."

M. Olney, Collector
August 30, 1944

THE FOUR MARYS

(Child 173)

Last night there were four Marys.
Tonight they'll be but three.
There was Mary Beaton and Mary Seaton
And Mary Carmichael and me.

O little did my mother think
When first she cradled me
That I would dee so far fra' hame
Or hang on the gallows tree.

They'll tie a napkin around my een
And they'll no let me see to dee
And they'll never let on to my father and mither
That I am away o'er the sea.

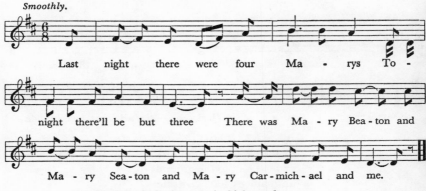

Last night there were four Marys To-
night there'll be but three There was Ma-ry Bea-ton and
Ma-ry Sea-ton and Ma-ry Car-mich-ael and me.

I wish I could lie in our ain kirk-yard
And neath the old yew tree
Where we pulled the gowans, and thread the rowans
My brothers and sisters and me.

Last night there were four Marys.
Tonight they'll be but three.
There was Mary Beaton and Mary Seaton
And Mary Carmichael and me.

Submitted by Miss Winifred S. Haskins of Savoy, Massachusetts. This ballad was taught to her when she was a small child, by her father's eldest sister—Eliza Ann (Haskins) Maynard.

H. H. F., Collector
August 5, 1934

PRINCE WILLIAM AND LADY MARGARET
(Child 74)

Prince William he courted Lady Margaret fair,
Determined to make her his wife;

They differed about a small trifle,
Which caused them both their life.

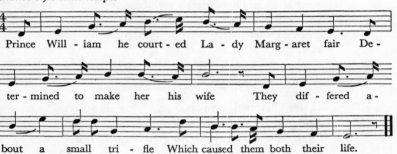

Prince Will - iam he court - ed La - dy Marg - aret fair De -

ter - mined to make her his wife They dif - fered a -

bout a small tri - fle Which caused them both their life.

Prince William he a-hunting went—
A-hunting for a deer—
But who should he meet but Margaret sweet,
A-walking to take the air.

He said that "I'm no man for you
And you're no girl for me—
Before three merry merry-more days—
My wedding you shall see."

She said: "If I'm no girl for you
And you're no man for me—
Before three merry merry-more days—
My funeral you shall see."

Lady Margaret she sat at her bow'ry window,
A-combing out her hair.
She saw Prince William and his bride pass by—
To a church they did repair.

Lady Margaret she threw down her ivory comb
And toss-ed back her hair.
She threw herself out of her bow'ry window,
And was seen alive no more.

Prince William he dream-ed a troublesome dream;
His dream it was not good;
He dreamed that his bowery was on fire,
And Margaret lay covered with blood;

Prince William arose and away he went—
And knock-ed at the ring;
There was none so ready as Margaret's brother—
To arise and let him in.

It was—"How do you do"—and "how do you do,"
And "how does fair Margaret do?"
"Fair Margaret is dead, lying on her cold bed—
And she died for the love of you."

"Go roll away the winding sheet—
That I may view the dead;
That I may kiss those cold pale lips
That once were cherry red.

"I'll kiss those cold pale lips again—
So they never will smile on me;
I made a vow by the powers above—
I'd marry none but she."

Lady Margaret she died on that same day—
Prince William he died on the morrow;
Lady Margaret she died of pure love alone—
Prince William he died of sorrow

Lady Margaret was buried by the salt sea side;
Prince William he was buried by her—;
And out of Lady Margaret's grave sprung a red rose
And out of Prince William's a brier.

They grew so high; they grew so tall;
They reached the mountain top;
They grew so high and they grew so tall—
They tied in a true-lover's knot.

Now all young people as you pass by,
And see where these two lovers do sleep.
Remember that pure love is better than gold—
Tho many many die for its sake.

ng by Mr. Asa Davis of Milton, Vermont, as learned from his father, Joel Davis, of
xbury, Vermont.

H. H. F., Collector
June 23, 1939

LADY MARGARET AND KING WILLIAM
(Child 74)

Lady Margaret was going to her high bow-er
All for to comb her hair.
She saw King William and his bride
A-going to church for prayers.

She threw down her ivory comb;
Threw back her yellow hair;
She threw herself from the high tow-er
And swore she would lie there.

Lady Margaret died in the middle of the night
When all the rest were asleep.
Her spirit left her fair bodee
And stood at William's feet.

"Oh, how do you like your bed," said she,
"And how do you like your sheets
And how do you like that fair la-dee
That in your arms does sleep?"

"Well do I like my bed," said he,
"And well do I like my sheets
But better do I like that fair la-dee
That stands at my bed's feet."

"I had a woeful dream," said she
"I hoped it never prove true—
I dreamed our cellar was filled with white wine,
Lady Margaret died for you."

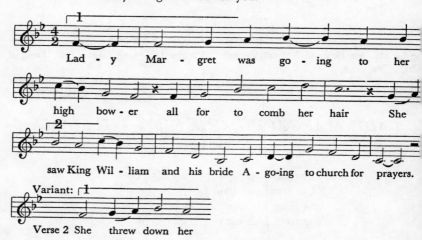

Lad - y   Mar - gret   was   go - ing   to   her

high   bow - er   all   for   to   comb   her   hair   She

saw King Wil - liam   and   his   bride   A - go-ing   to church for   prayers.

Variant:
Verse 2 She   threw down her

Variant:
Verse 3 Spir - it
Verse 8 None - so

"That is a woeful dream," said he,
"I hope it'll never prove true,
But I'll go up to the high bower
A-member days anew."

King William went to the high bower;
He knocked so loud at the ring.
There was none so ready as her own brother was
To arise and let him in.

"O is she in the kitchen," said he,
"Or is she in the hall,
Or is she in the long chamber—
The upper room of all?"

"She is not in the kitchen," said he,
"Nor is she in the hall.
But she is in the long chamber dead
With her face turned to the wall."

He folded down the milk-white sheets
That were spread up over her head
And there he saw both black and yellow
Where it used to be white and red.

Lady Margaret she died in the middle of the night.
Sweet William he died on the morrow.
Lady Margaret died for pure good love;
Sweet William he died for sorrow.

Lady Margaret was buried in the high church yard;
Sweet William was buried there beside her.
And out of Lady Margaret's breast grew a rose
And out of Sweet William's a briar.

They grew 'til they grew to the high church top
Where they could not grow any higher.
There they tied themselves in a true lover's knot
And they died away together.

Mr. George J. Edwards says, in giving this song in typewritten form, that it is "just as
always used it, and as I always heard it, with the one exception. I have omitted th
word 'little' immediately preceding the name 'Mottha Grow' wherever it occurs in th
piece. It always seemed to me that the words crowded the music (if that is a proper w
to express what I mean). I also did not like the impression the word conveyed as
seemed to me rather to belittle the person to whom it is attached and also to give
mental picture of a boy or youth, instead of a man."

H. H. F., Collect
July 27, 1933

LORD ARNOLD

(Child 81)

It was on one fine, one fine holiday,
The finest day in the year,
That Mottha Grow to the church did go
The Holy Word to hear.
The Holy Word to hear.

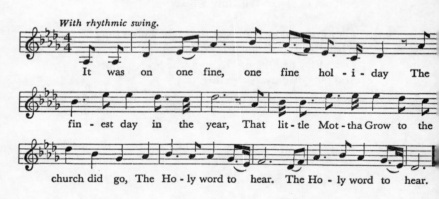

(Repeat last line in each verse)

The ladies fine, they all came in,
In satin and in blue.
The last of them all was Lord Arnold's wife,
The finest of the whole crew.

She looked around, she looked around,
She look-ed him upon,

Saying, "Mottha Grow, to my home must go,
And along with me shall come."

"I dare not, I dare not," said Mottha Grow,
"I dare not for my life,
For I know by the rings on your fingers,
That you are Lord Arnold's wife."

"And what if I am Lord Arnold's wife,
And what is that to thee?
Lord Arnold has gone to the Hampshire Court,
King Henry for to see."

A little foot page, a-standing near,
Heard all they had to say,
Thought, "I will tell Lord Arnold of this
Before the break of day."

"O, gold your head shall crown," Lady Arnold said,
"And silver your feet shall be,
If you will not tell Lord Arnold of what was said
Between Mottha Grow and me."

"O, gold will not crown my head," said he,
"Nor your silver will I take,
But I will tell Lord Arnold of this
Ere another day shall break."

He had many long miles to go
And some of them he ran,
And when he came to a broken bridge,
He down on his breast and swam.

And when he came to the Hampshire Court,
So loudly he did ring,

And none so ready as Lord Arnold himself
To arise and let him in.

"Are either of my towers burned,
Or is my castle won,
Or is my fair lady brought to bed,
With a daughter or a son?"

"There are neither of your towers burned,
Nor is your castle won,
Neither is your fair lady brought to bed
With a daughter or a son."

"What news, what news, my little foot page,
What news have you brought to me?"
"I have brought you the news that Mottha Grow
Is at home with your fair lady."

"If this be a lie," Lord Arnold, he said,
"That you have told to me,
I will have a wooden gallows made,
And hanged you shall be."

"If this be a lie," said the little foot page,
"That I have brought to thee,
You need not have a wooden gallows made,
But hang me on a tree."

"If this be true," Lord Arnold said,
"That you have told to me,
I have an estate in Northumberland
Which thy reward shall be."

Lord Arnold he summoned his merry men all,
By ones, by twos and by threes,
He ordered them not a drum should be beat,
Nor a bugle sounded be.

But there was one of Lord Arnold's men
Who loved his lady well,
He raised his bugle to his lips
And he sounded it loud and shrill.

"Hark, O hark!" said Mottha Grow,
"What's that I think I hear?
Methinks I hear Lord Arnold's bugle horn,
A-sounding in my ear.

"And ever as the bugle blows
It seems to me to say,
'Arise and dress ere its too late,
And away, Mottha Grow, away.' "

"Lie still, lie still, my Mottha Grow,
And keep me from the cold,
It is nothing but a shepherd boy
A-driving his sheep to the fold."

Lord Arnold he strode through the castle halls
And opened the door so wide.
They did not know Lord Arnold had come
Till he stood by their bedside.

"How do you like my bed," Lord Arnold said,
"And how do you like my sheets,
And how do you like my lady so fair
Who lies at your side so sweet."

"I like your bed very much," said he,
"I also like your sheets,
But much better do I like Lady Arnold so fair,
Who lies at my side so sweet."

"Arise, arise, you Mottha Grow,
And put your clothing on,

For I'll never have it said in Old England
That I slew a naked man."

"Must I arise?" said Mottha Grow,
"And fight you for my life,
While you have a glittering sword by your side
And I have not a knife?"

"Yes, I have a sword here at my side
And others in their place.
You shall have the best one of them
And I will take the worst.

"And you shall have the first full blow,
And strike it like a man.
I will have the next full blow
And I'll kill you if I can."

Mottha Grow he had the first full blow.
It wounded Lord Arnold sore.
Lord Arnold had the next full blow,
Mottha Grow could strike no more.

Lord Arnold then he looked around,
He look-ed him upon,
Saying, "I have killed the handsomest man
That ever the sun shone on."

Lord Arnold he took his lady by the hand
And sat her on his knee,
Saying, "Which do you like the very best now,
This Mottha Grow or me."

"Very well do I like your cherry cheeks,
Very well do I like your chin,
Better, much better do I like that Mottha Grow
Than Lord Arnold and his whole kin."

Lord Arnold he took his lady by the hand
He led her o'er the plain,
She never spoke another full word,
For he split her head in twain.

Sing on, sing on, ye nightengale,
Sing on, sing on, ye sparrow,
Lord Arnold has slain his wife to-day
And he shall be hung to-morrow.

A fragment as given by George J. Edwards of Burlington, Vermont.

H. H. F., Collector
November 1, 1933

THE ROSE OF ENGLAND
(Child 166)

Throughout a garden green and gay
A seemly sight it was to see.
The flowers flourished, fresh and gay
And birds did sing melodiously.

In the midst of the garden there sprung a tree
Which tree was of a mickle price.
Thereupon sprang a rose so red
The goodliest that e'er sprung on.

Given by Mr. George J. Edwards at Burlington, Vermont. This has been handed down
in his Northumbrian family for many generations.

H. H. F., Collector
May 24, 1934

THE TROOPER AND THE TURK
(Child 266)

John Thomson fought against the Turks,
In a country far away
From Scotland's shore, and bonny braes
And from his lady gay.

Three years and more he had been gone
From home, and lady fair;
Now this young chieftain sat alone
His mind on Scotland far.

He thought of his own childhood days,
And the happy hours he spent
When as a youth, o'er moor and fen
His wandering footsteps bent.

It happened once upon a day,
As he was walking down to the sea,
He espied his lady, in rich array,
As she was riding o'er the lea.

"What brought you here, my dear," he said,
"So far from friends and home?
Why did you not let me know, that it
Was your desire to come?"

"I pondered long, dear John," she said,
"E'er I made my mind to come;
I longed for your fair face to see,
It was that which lured me from our home."

For some days she did stay with him,
And seemed a loving wife to be,
"Then farewell for a time," she said.
For home again she must away.

He gave her jewels that were rare,
Set with pearls and precious stones,
Saying, "Beware of robbers bold,
That are on the way as you go home.

"You'll take the road, my lady fair,
That leads you far across the lea,

That will take you from the Turkish plain
Which is the home of base Vallentree."

These two did part with heavy hearts,
And, as he thought, she was going home.
Instead, she crossed the Turkish plain
And to base Vallentree she's gone.

When a full twelve months had passed,
John Thomson had thought wondrous long;
He wrote a letter to his brother then,
And sealed it well with his own hand.

He sent it with a vessel small,
That then was quickly going to sea
And sent it on to Scotland fair
And inquired about his gay lad-ee.

But the answer he received from home
Did grieve his heart right sore,
None of her friends had seen her there
For a year and something more.

Then he put on a palmer's weed,
And took a pike-staff in his hand,
And to the castle of Vallentree
Slowly his sorrowful way did wend.

And when within the hall he came,
He heavily on his staff did lean;
"If ye be the lady of this hall
Some of your bounty give to me."

"What news, what news, good man," said she,
"And from what country have you come?"
"I'm lately come from Grecian plains
Where camps some of the Scotch army."

"If you be come from Grecian plains
Some other news I'll ask of thee,
Regarding one of the chieftains there,
Has he lately seen his fair lad-ee?"

"It's a full twelve months and something more,
Since they did part on the Grecian plain;
And now this chieftain has begun to fear
That some of his foes have captured her."

"He has not taken me by force," quoth she,
"It was of my own free will,
He may tarry in the fight
But here I mean to tarry still.

"And if John Thomson you chance to see,
Tell him I wish him very well,
But his wife I can no longer be,
For now I love another man."

He then threw off his strange disguise,
Laid by the mask that he had on,
Saying, "Hide me now, my dearest wife,
For Vallentree will soon be home."

"For the love I bore you once,
I'll strive to hide you, if I can;"
She led him down to the cellar dark,
Where he saw many a newly slain man.

But he had not long in the cellar been
When a sound outside, caused him to fear.
It was the tread of many feet
As through the gates came Vallentree.

He greeted her with affection then
And said, "It's time that we should dine.

Bring forth from your most bountiful store,
And serve us with both bread and wine.

"That chief of the Scots, our dreaded foe
Who from the field has made us flee,
Ten thousand guineas in gold, I'd give
If I his face were permitted to see."

"If I produce this Scotchman bold
And cause him to before thee stand,
Will you surely, keep to me, your word
And pay this price into my hand?"

Then from the cellar she brought the chief,
And he came on most dejectedly.
The Turk then paid the price agreed,
And unto the chieftain he did say,

"I have thee in my power, now
And I shall work my will on thee;
But, if things were changed be-twixt us both
What would you do unto me?"

"If I had you, as you have me,
I'll tell you what I would do," he said,
"I would cause your own hand to arrange the tree
And hang you up in yon green-wood."

Sent by Mr. George J. Edwards of Burlington, Vermont, as it came down through the Douglas branch of his family. He writes: "Rosslyn Woods (as my grandfather used to spell it) was very near to the famous Roslin Castle, one of the famous old castles of Scotland." Mr. Edwards has given a dictaphone record of his singing of this song to the Archive. I think in the following text Vermont is due congratulations from all American collectors. The singer knew this ballad in his family tradition as the "Edward Ballad." Scholars recognize several verses common to Child versions of "The Twa Brothers" (Child 49). Its final verse resembles that of "Lizzie Wan" (Child 51).

H. H. F., Collector
January 22, 1934

EDWARD BALLAD

(Child 13)

It was in the Mid-Lothian Country,
Up near the Pentland hills,
Two brothers met one summer's day
To test their strength and skill.

Edward was the eldest one,
And John was the younger man;
They were equally matched in every way
To try what valor can.

"Shall we go to the school grounds?
Or will we remain at the Hall?
But, better we go to the greenwood,
To see which of us must fall."

"No, we'll not go to the school grounds,
Nor will we remain at the Hall,
But we will go to Roslyn woods
To see which of us will fall."

They struggled long for the mastery,
Till shadows told the end of the day,
When Edward waxed wroth at his failure,
And with his sword did his brother slay.

"Brother, raise me up and help me to walk;
Take me to yon stream so fair;
Wash the blood from out my wounds
So they will bleed no more."

He raised his brother upon his feet,
And helped him to the stream so fair.
Frantically he bathed his bloody wounds,
But they bled more and more.

"Now, brother, I know that I must die,
And I conjure you ere I go,
That you will not tell the folks at home
How this happened, nor let them know.

"Now lift me up, upon your back,
And take me to the churchyard fair;
Dig my grave both broad and deep
And lay my body there.

"You will place my arrows at my head;
My bow put at my feet;
My sword and buckler at my side
As though I were asleep.

"When you go home to my true love,
She'll ask for her lover John;

Say you left me in the churchyard fair
But you fear I'll never come home.

"When you go home to our sister,
She'll ask for her brother John;
Tell her I've gone to Stirling Carse
To see the king upon his throne.

"When you go home to our parents,
They'll ask you, 'Where is John?'
Tell them I'm at the Abbot's house
Studying there alone."

When he came home to John's true love,
She asked for her lover John.
He said, "I left him in the fair churchyard
And I fear he will never come home."

When he came home to his sister,
She asked for her brother John;
He told her he had gone to the Carse of Stirling
To the king upon his throne.

When he came home to his parents,
They asked for their son John;
"I left him at the Abbot's school
To study there alone."

"What blood is that on thy coat front, Edward?
It's as red as it can be."
"It's the blood of my great hawk
That uncle gave to me."

"Hawk's blood was never so red, son;
Come, and tell the truth to me."
"It is the blood of my greyhound, mother,
He would not run for me."

"That's not the blood of a hound, son;
That is very plain to see,
Is it not the blood of thy brother John?
Come, and tell the truth to me."

"It is the blood of brother John
O mother! Woe is me;
I slew him in a fit of rage,
Now the truth I have told to thee.

"You have always told me, mother,
Eldest sons must ne'er give in,
The family name and title
Must always be sure to win."

"What penance will you do, son,
To wipe away the stain?"
"I'll sail away across the seas,
And never come back again."

"What will you leave your wife and son,
If you sail beyond the sea?"
"I'll leave them my towers and hall, mother,
Which mean nothing now to me."

"What will you leave your mother, Edward,
Who has been so fond of thee?"
"I'll leave with her the memory of
Wrong counsel given me."

"When will you return, my son?
I shall long thy face to see."
"When the sunlight and moonbeams meet on the green,
And that will never be."

As sung by Miss Edith Ballenger Price of Newport, Rhode Island. Learned about 1910 when a small child, from the singing of a friend in Amherst, Massachusetts.

M. Olney, Collector
October 8, 1945

EDWARD

(Child 12)

"How came this blood on your shirt sleeve,
   O dear love, tell me, me, me?"
"It is the blood of my old gray hound
That traced that fox for me, me, me,
   that traced that fox for me."

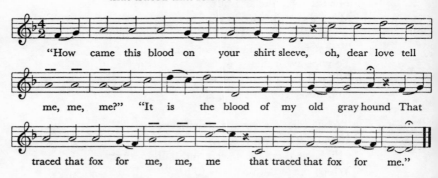

"How came this blood on your shirt sleeve, oh, dear love tell me, me, me?" "It is the blood of my old gray hound That traced that fox for me, me, me that traced that fox for me."

"It does look too pale for the old gray hound,
   O dear love, tell me, me, me—
It does look too pale for the old gray hound
That traced that fox for thee, thee, thee,
   that traced that fox for thee."

"How came this blood on your shirt sleeve,
   O dear love, tell me, me, me?"
"It is the blood of my old gray mare
That ploughed that field for me, me, me,
   that ploughed that field for me."

"It does look too pale for the old gray mare,
   O dear love, tell me, me, me—

It does look too pale for the old gray mare
That ploughed that field for thee, thee, thee,
　　that ploughed that field for thee."

"How came this blood on your shirt sleeve,
　　O dear love, tell me, me, me?"
"It is the blood of my brother-in-law
That went away with me, me, me,
　　that went away with me."

"And it's what did you fall out about,
　　O dear love, tell me, me, me?"
"About a little bit of bush
That never would have growed to a tree, tree, tree,
　　that never would have growed to a tree."

"And it's what will you do now, my love,
　　O dear love tell me, me, me?"
"I'll set my foot into yonders ship
And sail across the sea, sea, sea—
　　and sail across the sea!"

"And it's when will you come back again,
　　O dear love, tell me, me, me?"
"When the sun sets into yonders sycamore tree
And that will never be, be, be—
　　and that will never be!"

s sung by Mr. Jonathan Moses of Orford, New Hampshire.

H. H. F., Collector
June 26, 1942

JOHNNY SCOTT

(Child 99)

Young Johnny wrote a broad letter
And sealed it with his hand
He sent it to his own true love

In spite of Old England.
He sent it to his own true love
In spite of old England.

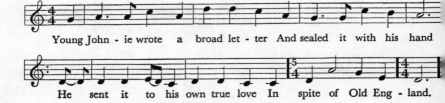

Young John-ie wrote a broad let-ter And sealed it with his hand
He sent it to his own true love In spite of Old Eng-land.

This fair maid wrote a broad letter
And sealed it with her ring.
She sent it to her Johnny Scott
In Scotland where he's been.

(*Etc.—Repeat last two lines.*)

When young John received this broad letter,
A sorry man was he.
He says, "I must go to old England again
To relieve that fair lady."

Then up speaks one of Johnny's men,
Lie low at Johnny's knee.
"Five hundred of my faith-life guards
Shall bear you companee."

The very first town that they rode through,
The trumpets they did sound;
The very next town that they rode through,
The drums did beat all 'round.

Then he rode up to the king's door
And wheeled his horses about.
And who did he spy but his own true love
At the window looking out.

"Come down, come down, my dear," he says,
"And talk awhile with me."
"I can't come down, my dear," she says,
"For the king has bolted me.

"My doors they are all bolted up;
My windows 'round about;
My feet they are in fetters strong.
My dear; I can't get out."

Then he rode up to the king's door
And knocked so loud at the ring
And none but so ready as the king himself
For to rise and let him in.

"O are you the Duke of Cumbritland,
Or aught, the British King,
Or are you now my bastard son
Who late-lie has stepped in?"

"I'm not the Duke of Cumbritland
Nor aught the British King
But I am a son of the worthy knight
And Johnny Scott is my name."

"Then if your name be Johnny Scott
As I suppose it be,
To-morrow morning 'fore the clock strikes eight,
You shall hang upon a tree."

Then the king prepared a tellyant man
And a bloody stout fellow was he.
He wore two sprands acrost his breast
And betwixt his shoulders, three.

Then up speaks one of Johnny's men
Lie-low at Johnny's knee,

"Before we'll see our master slain,
We'll fight all manfully."

Then the king with all his merry men
Went down upon the plain;
The queen with all her merry maids,
For to see fair Johnny slain.

Young John saluted this tellyant man;
Jumped on him and explained;
"Is there any more of your English dogs
That you vain-lie would have slain?"

"Oh, I'll give you half of my gold
And half of my gear,
If you'll return to old Scotland green
And leave my daughter here."

"I wants none of your gold," he says,
"I wants none of your gear,
But I will have my own true love
For I think I've bought her dear."

Sung by Mr. Jonathan Moses of Orford, New Hampshire, as learned from his father.
M. Olney, Collecto
July 3, 1942

SQUIRE RELANTMAN

(Child 93)

(*Last two lines repeated*)

Squire Relantman was a fine mason
    As ever you see;
He built a fine castle,
    Lord Nelson paid none.
He built a fine castle,
    Lord Nelson paid none.

Lord Nelson was a-going
    for to sail far away,
He told his fair lady
    for to keep her own room.

Squire Re - lant-man was a fine mas-on As ev - er you see; He built a fine cas - tle Lord Nel - son got none. He built a fine cas - tle Lord Nel - son got none.

(Repeat last line in each verse)

Lord Nelson he started
    and he sailed far away;
Kitchen windows being left open,
    Squire Relantman crept in.

"O where is Lord Nelson
    or is he within?"
"He has sailed far away."
    said this fair maid unto him.

"O where is his lady
    or is she within?"
"She is locked in her chamber,"
    said this fair maid unto him.

"O how can I get to her
    or how can I get in?"
"Stick a pin in her baby,"
    says this fair maid unto him.

Squire Relantman rocked the cradle
    while this fair maid she did sing,
And out of his cradle
    his heart's blood did spin.

"I cannot please your baby,
    I cannot please him on the key,
I cannot please your baby,
    you must come down and see."

"How can I come down
    so late in ther night
While there's no candles aburning
    nor no fire light?"

"Although it is late,
    so late in ther night
There is two candles a-burning
    and a good fire light."

This lady she started
    her baby for to see;
Squire Relantman he met her
    and he brought her upon her knee.

"O spare but my life
    two hours or three,
You shall have my daughter Betsey,
    fair a queen as you've seen."

"Daughter Betsey, daughter Betsey,
    go on the towers so high
And see if your own dear father
    ain't a-riding thereby."

Daughter Betsey, daughter Betsey
    Went on the towers so high,

There she saw her own dear father
    a-riding there by.

"O father, onward father
    O ride without speed,
Squire Relantman's killed your own son,
    your fair lady and me."

Squire Relantman was hung
    on the gallis so high;
This fair maid she was burned
    to a stake there nearby.

ıng by Mr. Charles Fennimore in Bridgewater, Maine, as his father used to sing it.

H. H. F. and M. Olney, Collectors
September 26, 1941

THE BLIND BEGGAR'S DAUGHTER

There was a blind beggar from Bethelhem town,
He had but one daughter of fame and renown;
She was handsome, well-featured in ev'ry degree
And the people all called her "Sweet Bone-y Betsey."

As Betsey was a-walking along the highway,
She met with an angel, unto her did say,
"It's in some king's palace, your entertainment might be
And happy is the young man gets bonny Betsey."

The first came courting Betsey was a squire so fine;
He came courting Betsey the most of his time.
"My lands and my freeholds, I'll give all to thee,
If you'll grant me your favour, sweet bonny Betsey."

Then the next came courting Betsey was a captain so fine.*
He came courting Betsey the most of his time.

---

* First said "so great," then changed it to "so fine."

"My ships on the ocean I will resign unto thee,
If you'll grant me your favour, sweet bonny Betsey."

Smoothly, narrative manner.

There was a blind beg-gar from Beth-el-hem town.

He had but one daugh-ter of fame and re-nown;

She was hand-some, well feat-ured in ev-'ry de-gree

And the peo-ple all called her "Sweet Bone-y Bet-sey."

Then the next came courting Betsey was a merchant so fine,
He came courting Betsey the whole of his time.
"All my gold and my silver, I will give all to thee,
If you'll tell me who's your father, sweet bonny Betsey."

"Now it's for my old father, he's very well known;
He is a blind beggar from Bethelhem town.
His marks and his tokens to you I will tell.
He is led by a dog with a chain and a bell."

"O hold," says the squire, "It's her I won't have."
"O hold," says the captain, "It's her I don't crave."
"O hold," say-ed the merchant, "If a beggar you be,
You're welcome now to me, sweet bone-y Betsey."

And then her old father, he stood in the door.
"Don't reflect on my daughter because she is poor;

Because she's not dressed in her silks and fine pearls,
On her I'll draw spangles. She's my bone-y brown girl."

The spangles were drawn and she knelt to the ground.
The beggar man laid down his five thousand pounds.
When the merchant had laid down the last of his store,
The beggar man laid down five thousand pounds more.

.s sung by Mrs. Lena Bourne Fish of East Jaffrey, New Hampshire. Mrs. Fish says that
is has been sung in her family for many years.

M. Olney, Collector
May 9, 1940

THE CASTLE BY THE SEA
(Child 4)

"Arise, O arise, my lady fair,
For you my bride shall be,
And we will dwell in a sylvan bower,
In my castle by the sea.

"Then bring along your marriage fee,
Which you can claim today,
And also take your swiftest steed,
The milkwhite and the gray."

The lady mounted her milkwhite steed;
He rode the turban gray,
They took the path by the wild seashore,
Or so I've heard them say.

As she saw the wall of the castle high,
They looked so bleak and cold;
She wished she'd remained in Boston town,
With her ten thousand pounds in gold.

He halted by the wild seashore,
Saying, "My bride you shall never be,
For six fair maidens I've drown-ed here;
The seventh you shall be.

With spirit.

A - rise, O a - rise, My la - dy fair, For

you my bride shall be, And we will dwell in a

Var. B.

syl - van bower In my cas - tle by the sea.

Var. A.

Verses: 7. is   a   dis - grace   to
        8. took   him   in   her
        9. six   fair   maid-ens you've
        10. rode   'till   she came   to

Var. B.

Verses: 2. swift - est steed   the
        3. wild   sea - shore   or
        9. drown - ed   here   go

"Take off, take off your scarlet robes,
And lay them down by me;
They are too fine and too costly
To rot in the briny sea."

"Then turn your face to the water side,
And your back to yonder tree;
For it is a disgrace to any man,
An unclothed woman to see."

He turned his face to the waterside,
And his back to the lofty tree;
She took him in her arms so bold,
And flung him into the sea.

"Lie there, lie there, you false young man,
And drown in place of me,
If six fair maidens you've drown-ed here,
Go keep them company."

She then did mount her milkwhite steed,
And led the turban gray,
And rode till she came to Boston town,
Two hours before it was day.

Mr. Jack MacNelly of Siberia, out of Staceyville, Maine, recalled some of this ballad.
                                                H. H. F., Collector
                                                July 13, 1940

THE KING'S THREE QUESTIONS
(Child 45)

Come all you folks and I'll make you merry
When I tell you the story of the Bishop of Canterbury.

(He was arrested for having too much money—more than the king.)

"First you must tell me without any doubt
How long I'll be traveling this world about."

"And get up with the sun and go 'round with the same
And four and twenty hours will bring you back again."

"The second you must tell me what I am worth."

"The Lord was sold for thirty pieces of silver
So you must be worth thirty-three
For probably you are worth three pennies more than he."

"The third you must tell me what I think."

"You think I'm the Bishop of Canterbury
And I nawthin but his hired man."

This song was jointly remembered by Mr. Elmer George and his sisters, Mrs. Cora
Johnson and Mrs. Myra Daniels, in East Calais, Vermont.

H. H. F., Collector
July 29, 1933

LUMBERMAN'S ALPHABET

A is for axes that you may all know;
And B is for boys that make them all go;
C is for choppers so early begun
And D is for danger we often stand in.

CHORUS:

'Tis merry, 'tis merry, 'tis merry are we
No mortal on earth, so happy as we.
A derry, Lo derry, Ring derry dum.
Give us shantymen's grog and there'll
        nothing go wrong.

E is the echo that through the woods rang:
F is the foreman, head one of our gang;
G is the grindstone so merrily goes round
And H is the handle, so smoothly 'tis worn.

I is the Iron that mark-ed the pine:
J is the Jov-al that's never behind;
K is the keen edge our axes we keep
And L is the lice that over us creep.

M is the moss we patch-ed the cracks
And N is the needle we patch-ed our pants;

O is the owl that hooteth at night
And P is the pine that always falls right.

Q is the quarrel we never allow;
R is the river we float our logs down
S is the sleds so stout and so strong
And T is the teams that go jog 'em along.

U is the use we put our teams to;
V is the valley we draw our logs through;
W is the woods we leave in the spring
And this is all I am going to sing.

rs. Sullivan of Springfield, Vermont, sang this lamenting song, which must have
iginated a few centuries ago.

THE LOWLANDS O HOLLAND

When I was newly married
And in my marriage bed
In came a bold sea captain
And to me he boldly said,
"Arise, arise, my new married man
And come along with me
To the lowlands low of Holland
To fight your enemy."

The love that I have chosen
With him I will be content
The salt sea shall be frozen
Before that I repent,
Repent it I shall never
Until the day I die
But the lowlands o Holland
Lies between my love and me.

"My love he built a bunny ship
And set her on the main
With twenty four brave mariners
To sail around the seas.
But the stormy winds did arise
And the raging seas did roar
And true love and his bunny ship
Returned to land no more.

"There shall no mantle cross my back,
No comb go in my hair,
Neither shall coal nor candle light
Shine in my bower fair
Nor shall I choose another love
Until the day I die
Since the low lowlands o Holland
Lies between my love and me."

"Nor hold your tongue, my daughter dear,
Be still and bide content.
There's other lads in Galoway
Ye need nor to lament."
"There is no lad in Galoway—
No other lad for me—
I ne'er loved a lad but one
And he's drowned in the sea."

Furnished by Mrs. George Tatro of Springfield, Vermont, as handwritten by her grandmother's cousin, Louisa Nutting Bradley, of East Berkshire, Vermont. Copied literati
et punctatim.

H. H. F., Collect
June 19, 1939

MULBERRY DISASTER

Come all ye good people of every degree;
And listen with attention one moment to me,

For a sorrowful story I mean to relate,
Of a mournful disaster that happened of late.

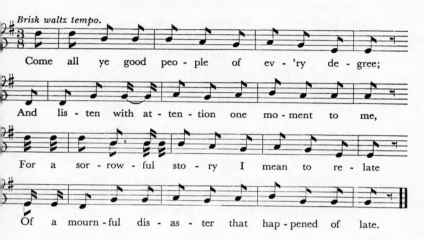

Brisk waltz tempo.

Come all ye good peo - ple of ev - 'ry de - gree;

And lis - ten with at - ten - tion one mo - ment to me,

For a sor - row - ful sto - ry I mean to re - late

Of a mourn - ful dis - as - ter that hap - pened of late.

Oh Mulberry trembled at that awful stroke;
Consider the voice of Jehoval that spoke.
To teach us we are mortal, and exposed to death;
And subject each moment to yield up our breath.

Oh, reader, these coffins exhibit to view
A striking example tis mournfully true.
To shew thee death will be thy certain doom.
For shortly thy body will enter the tomb.

Twas on Friday, the twelveh of December, so cold.
The year eighteen hundred as I have been told,
The wind blowing high, and the rain beating down
The vessel arrived at Mulberry town.

The anchor being cast and the sails torn away,
All hands for the shore prepared start away,
Down into those boats they all did repair,
And for the shore prepared to steer.

But mark their sad fortune oh mournful indeed;
No man can hinder what God has decreed.
For the counsel of heaven on that fatal day;
By death in an instant called a number away.

For a number of men in their health and prime
Were called out of this world in an instant of time,
For the boat turning over plunged them all in the deep;
And five out of seven in death fell asleep.

Those sorrowful tidings were carried straightway
To those friends and relations without more delay,
But oh, their lamenting, no tongue can express
Nor point out their sorrow, their grief and distress.

Three widows bereft in sorrow to mourn;
The loss of their husbands no more to return,
Also a great number of orphans, we hear,
Lamenting the great loss of their parents so dear.

Also a young damsel, making great mourn;
For the loss of her lover, no more to return,
For the day of their nuptial appointed had been;
In the hands of sweet wedlock these lovers to join.

Their bodies being found, their corpse conveyed home,
The Sabboth day following were prepared for the toomb.
Their bodies in their coffins were laid side by side,
In Malborrough meeting house alley so wide.

A numerous concourse of people straightway;
Attended with sorrow that awful day,
To see the remains of their neighbors so dear,
And join their relation in a friendly tear.

Their bodies being found, their corpse were conveyed,
To the cold cavern of earth they were laid,

And now we must leave them to moulder to dust;
Until the ressurection of the just and the unjust.

Unto the widows and mourners overwhelmed with grief,
May we all trust in God to grant you relief,
He will ease all your sorrows and soothe all your pains;
And finally take you home in glory to reign.

Come all ye that are living and know that you must die,
I pray take warning by this tragedy,
That when death shall call you to close up your eyes,
Your souls may be happy with Christ in the skies.

. . Stories, admittedly, are localized! And in the transplantings we find such
hanges as in "The Alphabet Song" in lumber camps beginning:

> "Give us shantymen's grog
> And there'll nothing go wrong"

om its original:

> "Give the sailor-boy grog, etc."

lover rides on a horse in one part of a country where there are hills—in
nother where there is a sea—he comes in a boat in the very same story. Melons
become pumpkins in different countries. I have recently heard the very windy
music of two East Indian instruments, the Sarode and the Israj. The latter,
highly polished neem wood, had an augmented resonance in a hollowed
umpkin attached to the neck of the instrument. "Gourd?" I had asked.
No, pumpkin."

Nearby had stood Joan and Betty Rayner,* two sisters who have studied
lk lore, in many nations, from its sources, combing manuscripts and ancient
lumes from medieval libraries. They entered the conversation, "That ex-
ains the Bengalese tale which speaks of pumpkins when we always expected
e words 'gourds.' "

---

* Directors of the Australian Children's Theatre—a traveling group of professional artists
ing drama, dance and music to the young.

They repeated the story found in India, which since has appeared in music hall minstrel version: A simple boy and his brother were walking across the field and saw a lot of pumpkins lying around. The simple boy said, "What are those?" His brother said, "They're mules' eggs. The mother mule sits on them for three weeks and then the baby mule comes out." So the simple boy took one home and sat on it for three weeks. When nothing happened at the end of that time the boy angrily threw the pumpkin at a tree—it broke into a thousand pieces and frightened a rabbit that was sitting on the other side of the tree. As the rabbit ran away the boy saw it and called out, "Hi, come back here, I'm your father!"

When the rabbit rushed away at the breaking up of the pumpkin it was as though I were meeting a ghost. For I was hearing the very early form of a story told me in recent years by a man from the Michigan lumber woods. Then, he was relating how the men had taken an Irish immigrant "for a ride." His story went this way: "Among the many things new to Pat, in our country, was a pumpkin. He was told it was a mare's egg. He became interested in the special foal it would hatch; and finally secured one. But it was a slippery pumpkin under his arm. Shortly it struck a rock at his feet, starting up a rabbit that rushed from the spot. Pat yelled wildly, "Stop my foal!"

Sometimes the pattern of a line is taken bodily. The old song, "The Lowlands of Holland," was known most poignantly to Mrs. Sullivan, a native of Ireland, living in Springfield, Vermont. To repeat the first verse:

"When I was newly married
And in my marriage-bed,
In came a bold sea-captain
And to me he boldly said,
'Arise, arise, my new married man
And come along with me
To the lowlands, low, of Holland
To fight your enemy.'"

Compare Mrs. Sullivan's verse with the following, which I came upon in Ellsworth, Maine, one autumn. It was about a woodsman, and a lumber boss John Ross:

"The night that I was married
Laying on my marriage-bed,
Up steps John Ross, that Irishman,
He stood at my bed-head
Saying, 'Arise, you lovely Irishman,
And come along with me
To the low, low lands of Chesuncook
For to swamp those logs for me.' "

When a tragedy strikes a community, and is made into song by way of
etailing the news, there is an apt folk-choice of wording and tunes. Here is
ne I ran upon in a text in the possession of Mrs. Ella Doten (now deceased)
f North Calais, Vermont. It was "written by Reuben Waters" after five out
f eighteen persons were drowned when their boat sprung a leak on Calais
'ond.* Here is its second verse:

"O, Calais did tremble at this awful stroke
And considered the voice of Jehovah had spoke
To teach us we're mortals, exposed to death
And subject each moment to yield up our breath."

he verse is almost identical with the song about "Mulberry Town," I had
ound in the papers of Mrs. George Tatro, of English descent, from Berkshire,
ermont, only there, "Mulberry trembled at that awful stroke" etc.

In the Pepys Collection, "The Unconstant Maiden or The Forsaken Young
Ian," which shows how a Devonshire damsel "Marry'd another while her
ver was come to London, to his great grief" uses:

"Here is a Ring of Gold, My dear, accept it.
'Tis for your sake alone, long have I kept it."

he same words appear a century later in a folk song current after Wolfe died
 the Plains of Abraham:

"Love, here's a diamond ring, a long time I've had it
For your sake alone, a long time I've kept it."

---

* *The New Green Mountain Songster,* p. 215, and *Vermont Chap Book,* p. 46.

Miss Marguerite Olney points out that a hymn she recorded, which begin

"Saw ye my Saviour?"

as Mrs. Jo Wilson, of Springfield, Vermont, sang it, is in a broadside of 177
beginning:

"Saw ye my mother?
Saw ye my father?
Saw ye my true love, John?"*

and ending as no hymn would ever have ended. When it is printed
Chappell, in 1829 in "Popular Music of the Olden Time," both have t
same tune.

Copied from the written back pages of an old receipt book belonging to Mrs. Char
L. Olney, Springfield, Vermont.
Copied literatim et punctatim.

M. O., Collect
February, 193

BRAVE WOLFE

Cheer up your hearts, young men, let nothing fright you,
Let not your courage fail, till after trial,
Nor let your fancy move, at the first denial.

Cheer up your hearts, young men, let noth-ing fright you
Let not your cour-age fail, till af-ter tri-al, Nor
let your fan-cy move, at the first de-ni-al.

* From *Vocal Music or the Songsters Companion,* Vol. 2, p. 36. Printed for Rob
Horsfield, at No. 22 in Ludgate Street, London, England.

I went to see my love only to woo her,
I went to gain her love, not to undo her,
Whene'er I spoke a word, my tongue did quiver,
I could not speak my mind, while I was with her.

Love, here's a diamond ring, long time I've kept it,
'Tis for your sake alone, that I have kept it,
When you the posy read, think on the giver,
Madam, remember me, or I'm undone forever.

Brave Wolfe then took his leave of his dear jewel
Most surely did she grieve, saying don't be cruel;
Said he, 'tis for a space that I must leave you,
Yet love, where'er I go, I'll not forget you.

So then this gallant youth did cross the ocean,
To free America from her invasion,
He landed at Quebec with all his party,
The city to attack, both brave and hearty.

Brave Wolfe drew up his men in form so pretty,
On the plains of Abraham, before the city,
There, just before the town, the French did meet them,
With double numbers, they resolved to beat them.

When drawn up in a line, for death prepared,
While in each other's face their armies stare,
So pleasantly brave Wolfe and Montcalm talked,
So martially between their armies walked.

Each man then took his post at their retire,
So then these numerous hosts began to fire,
The cannon on each side did roar like thunder,
And youth in all their pride was torn asunder.

The drums did loudly beat, colors were flying
Brave Wolfe began to wake as he lay dying,

He lifted up his head while guns did rattle
And to his army said, how goes the battle?

His aide-de-camp replied, "Tis in our favor,
Quebec with all her pride, we soon shall have her,
She'll fall into our hands with all her treasure;"
"Oh then," brave Wolfe replied, "I die with pleasure."

As sung by Mrs. Jo Wilson of Springfield, Vermont. Mrs. Wilson says that her fathe
sang this hymn to her over seventy years ago in New York State.

H. H. F., Collecto
June 24, 1940

SAW YE MY SAVIOUR

Saw ye my Saviour, saw ye my Saviour,
Saw ye my Saviour and Lord?
Oh, He died on Calvary, to atone for you and me,
And to purchase our pardon with blood.

Darkness prevaileth, darkness prevaileth,
Darkness prevaileth o'er the land.
Oh, the solid rocks were rent to creation's vast extent,
When the Jews crucified the God-man.

Jesus hung bleeding, Jesus hung bleeding,
Three dreadful hours in pain,
Crying, "Father, I have died, thus behold my hands and side,
To atone for them, pray thee forgive."

"I will forgive them, I will forgive them,
If they repent and believe;
Let them now return to me and be reconciled to Thee,
And full pardon they all shall receive."

We might as well point out here that in the song "Little Harry Huston"
occur these words:

> "The Jewess she did me wrong, wrong,
> The Jewess she did me wrong"

which phrase is vehemently sung in "Frankie and Johnny."

There is one outstanding example of repetitions occurring a century and
more apart. William Butler Yeats published "Down in the Salley Gardens" in
his collection of poems *Crossways* in 1889. A salley, in Ireland, is a water
willow. The poem is even more graceful with that in mind.

> "Down in the salley gardens my love and I did meet;
> She passed the salley gardens with little snow-white feet.
> She bid me take love easy, as the leaves grow on the tree;
> But I, being young and foolish, with her would not agree.
>
> "In a field by the river my love and I did stand,
> And on my leaning shoulder she laid her snow-white hand.
> She bid me take love easy, as the grass grows on the weirs;
> But I was young and foolish, and now am full of tears."

In a copybook now in the possession of the Baker Memorial Library at
Hanover, New Hampshire, is a folk song handwritten by Joseph Goffe, dated
1784 in Bedford, New Hampshire. Some twelve years ago a descendant,
Mrs. Charlotte Woodbury, living in nearby Manchester, copied for me the
way Mr. Goffe had penned "Down in Sally's Garden." We do not know how

old was the ballad when he learned it. Granted it came out of Ireland, b
1784 the word "salley" made to him no sense. Here are the stanzas literatim e
punctatim:

> It's down in Sally's Garden
> O there hangs Rosies three
> O there, I met a fair Maid
> who told to me her mind so free
> She bids me take love easy
> As leaves they do falls from the tree
> but I being young and Crazy
> Could not with her agree.

The rest of the song is included because of its inherent folk quality, thoug
only the first stanza parallels Yeats' poem.

> A Letter of Agreement
> I Sent unto my turtle Dove
> with many a kind Compliment
> and Seald it with a kiss of Love
> Saying if you Don't accept of this
> You will prove Cruel to my pain
> I Ne'er will be a Slave
> to your fair female Sex again.

> I wish I was in Ireland
> or Some Such Country of my own
> Where Girls I Could get plenty
> But here I Can't have None
> Where Girls they are So plentiful
> Although their portions be but Small
> Sweetheart I Could have Twenty
> Could I but Maintain them all.

> I wish I was in Liverpool
> and my true Love along with me
> And everything was fitted
> to Serve his Royal Majesty

Where Liquor is So plentiful
and flowing bowls on ev'ry Side
hard fortune Should not Daunt me
I'm young and the World is Wide.

To the naked eye as well as to the naked consciousness one poem is by a poet; one, by several generations of singers.

Oral tradition is not the same as printed tradition, but both may indicate a critical sensitivity and show the touch of a connoisseur. Singers savor old tales; they remedy a word to suit their fancy and breathe life upon it.

We come upon such re-fitted words as "inspective eyes" in Luther's "True Lover's Discussions," or "I asked of her an exclamation" in "Charming Sally Ann"* as sung by Elmer George of North Montpelier, Vermont; and "Is Willie a-dead or alive?" in "Mary and Willie" sung by Arthur Moore of Island Falls, Maine. Another well renovated word was used by Mrs. Ellen Sullivan, in "The Glen of Ahalough" where she sang of "a poor neglected midjutant."

Remarkable choices are made by some singers, admirably hewing the line. This, for instance, sung by a bedridden Irish woman in her version of "The Cherry Tree Carol":

"The highest branch bended, the lowest branch bowed,
Blessed Mary picked cherries *while* her apron could hold."**

Or this ancient, lamenting line from Child 106 as sung by Mrs. Belle Richards of Colebrook, New Hampshire:

" 'Twas all alone I dug his grave
And all alone in it him I laid,
While Christ was priest and I was clerk
I laid my love in the clay-cold earth."

I have looked through many regional collections as well as the monumental works of Professor Francis James Child and of Cecil Sharp but have not discovered the especial grief of this passage.

---

* *Garland of Green Mountain Song*, p. 42.
** *Country Songs of Vermont*, p. 48.

Probably Hanford Hayes, ex-foreman on log drives, who had known ⊂
many a drowning in that hazardous life, was satisfied to sing in "The Out
landish Knight":

> "He droop-ed high, he droop-ed low
> And turned to the top of the tide,"

though it was thus "worded" several generations before his time.

Lines of pure poetry sometimes bring to life both the tale itself and th
singer who made them up. This, for instance, in the possession of Mrs. Alic
Robie of Pittsburg, New Hampshire, from the manuscript version of "Th
House Carpenter":

> She went into her golden room
> And dressed in silk so fine;
> She turned around and around again
> For she shone like a diamond's bride.

And from the "Bonnie Earl of Murray":

> "O, long will this lady
> Look o'er the castle down,
> Ere she sees the Earl of Murray
> Come sounding through the town!"

It is one thing to imagine the bonnie Earl of Murray "soundin' throug
the toon"; another to think of Adam O'Gordon sweeping down from th
north with all the fury of clan-vengeance on a castle tower that even no
stands lonely in the countryside. The Lord was away, the Lady and her chil
easy prey to the marauder. Adam Gorman is a hideous story—but a rar
ballad. So it is included here as sung by Lily Delorme who ended her day
in Cadyville, New York. She learned it from her forebears of Starksbor
Vermont. . . .

sung by Mrs. Belle Richards in Colebrook, New Hampshire.

M. Olney, Collector
April 25, 1942

SWEET WILLIAM

(Child 106)

My father was a noble knight.
My mother was a lady bright,
And I myself a lady gay,
But now I wait as a servant boy.

Rhythmic - narrative manner.

My fath - er was a no - ble knight, My moth - er was a lad - y bright And I my - self was a lad - y gay But now I wait as a ser - vant boy.

My father built me a lovely bower.
It was as fine as any flower.
'Twas covered all o'er with the beautifulest green.
O such a bower scarce ere was seen.

My father matched me with a knight.
My stepmother owed me a dreadful spite.
She sent four robbers all in the night
To rob my bower and slay my knight.

'Twas all alone they did him kill,
And all alone they left him still.
There was nothing left to wrap him in
But the bloody sheet where my love was slain.

'Twas all alone I dug his grave
And all alone in it him I laid.
While Christ was priest and I was clerk
I laid my love in the clay-cold earth.

I saddled my horse and away did ride,
With sword and pistols by my side;
I cut off my hair and changed my name
From Ellen Fair to Sweet William.

I rode till I came to the king's high hall
And for my supper I did call.
I gave the porter a gay, gold ring
To carry my message unto the king.

The king came down and thus did say,
"What can you do, young man, I pray?
If you can do what I want you to,
I'll hire you for a year or two."

" 'Tis I can be your kitchen cook
Or I can be your stableman
Or I can be waiter all in your hall
And wait on the nobles as they call."

" 'Tis you shan't be my kitchen cook
Nor you shan't be my stableman,
But you shall be waiter all in my hall
And wait on the nobles as they call."

The king being gone one day from home,
There was no one there but the good old man.
Sometimes she sighed, sometimes she sang,
Sometimes the tears down her cheeks did run.

The king came home and thus did say,
"What news, what news, old man, I pray?"

"Good news, good news, my king," said he,
"Sweet William is a lady gay."

"Go bring me down a suit of silk—
It shall be white as any milk.
I'll dress her up in the silk so fine.
And make her rule over all that's mine."

As sung by Mr. Hanford Hayes of Staceyville, Maine. This is a fragment. Sung to Mrs. A. C. Beal and

H. H. F., Collector
September 21, 1940

THE OUTLANDISH KNIGHT

(Child 4)

There was a knight came from the Northland
And from the Northland came he.

"Bring me some of your father's gold
And some of your mother's fee;
Two of the best horses out of the stable
Where there stands thirty and three."

She leaped upon a milk-white steed
And he took a dapple-gray.
They rode till they came to the river's side
Three hours before it was day.

"Strip off, strip off your silks and gowns
And deliver them unto me.
I'm sure they are too costelee
To rot in the salt sea."

"If I must strip off my silks and gowns
You must turn your back to me

For it isn't becoming a robber like you
A naked woman to see."

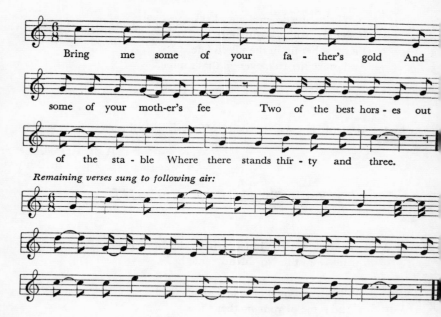

Bring me some of your fa - ther's gold And
some of your moth-er's fee Two of the best hors - es out
of the sta - ble Where there stands thir - ty and three.

Remaining verses sung to following air:

He turned his back unto her
A-viewing the leaves so green.
She caught him by the waist so small
And plunged him out into the sea.

He droop-ed high, he droop-ed low
And turned to the top of the tide.
Saying, "Reach me your hand, my pretty Pollee,
And I will make you my bride."

"Lie there, lie there, my false young man,
Lie there, lie there," cried she,
"Six maidens you have drownded here.
The seventh one drownded thee."

She leaped upon her milk-white steed
And led her dappled-gray.
She rode till she came to her own father's house
One hour before it was day.

The parrot being up in the treetops so high
And hearing the maiden, did say,
"What is the matter, my pretty Pollee,
You tarry so long before day?"

"O, hold your tongue, my pretty Polly.
Don't tell no tales upon me.
Your cage shall be made of the glittering gold
And hang upon yonder green tree."

The old man being up in the window so high
And hearing the parrot, did say,
"What is the matter, my pretty Pollee,
You prattle so long before day?"

"O nothing, O nothing," the parrot replied,
"O nothing, I'm sure it to be.
The cat is up in the window so high
And she is a-watching for thee."

"Well turned, well turned, my pretty Pollee,
Well turned, well turned," cried she,
"Your cage shall be made of the glittering gold
And the doors of ivory."

As copied from manuscript belonging to Mrs. Alice Robie of Pittsburg, New Hampshire
This manuscript originally belonged to her sister, Mrs. Luther, whose husband knew and
sang many of the old ballads. Copied literatim et punctatim.

M. Olney, Collector

THE YOUNG TURTLE DOVE

(Child 243)

Don't you see young turtle dove
That sits on yonder pine,
She is lamenting for her true love,
As I'm lamenting for mine.

I have returned from the salt, salt sea
And for to marry you,
And you are married to a house carpenter
And he is a fine young man.

She went into her golden room
And dressed in silk so fine;
She turned around and around again
For she shone like a diamond's bride.

She went unto her dear little babe
And gave it kisses three
Saying, Stay at home my dear little babe;
Keep your papa company.

They had not sail'd more than one or two weeks,
I am sure it was not three,
When this fair maid, she began to weep
And she wept most bitterly.

Why do you mourn for your house carpenter that you have left on shore?
I do not mourn for my house carpenter that I left on shore;
But I do mourn for my dear little babe
That I shall see no more.

They had not sailed more than two or three weeks,
I am sure it was not four,
Before the ship sank in the deep
And sank to use no more.

The following was copied from the written back pages of an old receipt book belonging to Mrs. Charles L. Olney, Springfield, Vermont.

M. Olney, Collector
February, 1939

EARL OF MURRAY

(Child 181)

Ye Highlands and ye Lowlands,
O! where have you been?
They have slain the Earl of Murray
And they laid him on the green!
They have slain the Earl of Murray
And they have laid him on the green!

Now woe be to thee Huntley!
And wherefore did you see?
I bade you bring him with you,
But forbade you him to slay.

(Repeat last two lines of each stanza)

He was a brave gallant,
And he rode at the ring,
And the Bonnie Earl of Murray
O! might have been a king!

He was a brave gallant
And he played at the glove;
And the Bonnie Earl of Murray,
O! he was the Queen's love!

O! long will this lady
Look o'er the castle down,
Ere she sees the Earl of Murray
Come sounding through the town.

From Mrs. Lily Delorme of Cadyville, New York, of Vermont parentage.

M. Olney, Collector
November, 1943

ADAM GORMAN

(Child 178)

'Twas 'round about the Martin-mass,
When north winds froze the lake,
Said Adam Gorman to his men,
"We must some castle take!"

Moderately fast, rhythmic.

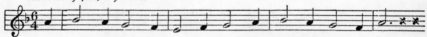

'Twas 'round a-bout the Mar-tin-mass When north winds froze the lake;

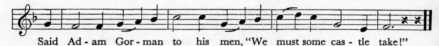

Said Ad-am Gor-man to his men, "We must some cas-tle take!"

"And what brave castle shall we take,
My merry men and me?
We will go strait to Towie House,
And see that fair ladee."

The lady from her castle wall
Looked o'er both dale and down,
When she beheld a troop of men,
Fast riding through the town.

"O see you not, my merry men all,
See you not what I see?

Methinks I see a troop of men;
I wonder who they be?"

She thought it was her loving lord,
Who homeward riding came.
It was the traitor, Adam,
Who feared not sin nor shame.

She had no sooner decked herself
In silken scarf and gown,
Than Adam Gorman, and his men,
Had close beset the town.

The lady went to her tow'r so high,
For she was in deep dismay;
To see if by fair speech she could
The traitor's purpose stay.

But when he saw the lady safe,
The gates and windows fast,
He fell into a deadly rage
And stormed at her aghast;

"Come down to me, thou lady gay,
Come down, come down to me;
This night thou shall be in my arms,
Tomorrow my bride shalt be."

"I'll not come down, thou false Gorman
I'll not come down to thee;
I'll not forsake my own dear lord,
Tho' he is far from me."—

"Give up thy house, thou lady fair,
Give up thy house to me!
Or I shall burn thyself therein,
With thy dear babies three."—

"I'll not give up, thou false Gorman.
Thy threatenings I deny.
If thou dost burn my babes and me,
Then, thou my lord, shall die (?)

"But reach and give me my pistol,
And charge with speed my gun,
For I must pierce that savage dog
Or we shall be undone."

She from the battlements took aim
As true as she could see;
Two bullets missed the traitor's heart,
One only grazed his knee.

"Now fire the house," cried false Gorman
Enraged with vengeful ire;
False lady thou shalt rue this deed,
When shrieking in the fire."—

"Woe unto thee, woe unto thee,
I paid thee well thy fee;
Why then pull out the ground wall stone
That lets in smoke to me?"

"That thou dids't pay my fee and hire,
Full well, I can't deny;
Yet now I'm Adam Gorman's man
I must obey or die."—

O then did speak her little son,
Upon his nurse's knee,
"O mother, dear, give up this house,
The smoke it smothers me."

"I would give all my gold, my child,
And likewise all my fee—

For one blast of the western wind,
To blow the smoke from thee:"

O then bespoke her daughter dear,
So slender, fair, and small,
"O roll me in a pair of sheets
And throw me o'er the wall."

They rolled her in a pair of sheets
And threw her o'er the wall,
But on the point of Gorman's spear
She got a deadly fall.

O lovely, lovely was her mouth:
Her cheeks were like the rose
And clear, clear was her yellow hair,
Whereon the red blood flows.

Then with his spear he turned her o'er
O how her face was wan!
"I might have spar'd that lovely face
To be some man's delight.—

"Prepare, prepare, my merry men all,
Ill tidings I do guess:
I cannot see that lovely face
So pale upon the grass."

"Who looks for grief, my master, dear,
Grief still will follow them:
Shall it be said that Gorman bold
Was daunted by this dame?"—

But when the lady saw the fire
Come flaming o'er her head,
She wept, and kissed her children dear;
"My babes will soon be dead."—

Then Gorman did his bugle blow
And said, "Away, away!
Since Towie House is all in flames,
We must no longer stay."

And then looked up her own dear lord,
As he came o'er the lea;
He saw his castle in a blaze
As far as he could see.

Then sorely did his mind misgave,
And his heart was full of woe:
"Put on, put on, my trusty men
As fast as you can go.

"For life and death, my trusty men,
Put on, put on, amain!
For he that doth the hindmost lag
Shall ne'er my favor gain."

Then some did ride, and some did run
No swifter flew the wind;
For each cried, "Woe upon the head
Of him who lags behind."—

But e'er the foremost could come up,
The flames had spread so wide,
The tender babes were burnt alive.
Their mother with them died.

Her lord did wildly rent his hair
And wept in woeful mood:
"Ah, traitors, for this cruel deed
You shall weep tears of blood."—

Full fast false Gorman he pursu'd
With many a bitter tear—

And in his cowardly own heart's blood
Revenged his lady dear.

. . The average singer accepts unquestioningly the old lines in the old tunes.
If they do not make sense, he makes his own sense. When the legend of
Margery Grey was taken up by the folk from verses written by Mrs. Julia
C. R. Dorr of Rutland, certain verbal changes were passed along by word of
mouth, in the region of the Connecticut Lakes. Tragically Robert Grey
approaches the cabin:

> "Black and desolate it stood;
> Cold the hearth and windows ralist
> In their stillest solitude."*

The singer as a child had learned the song from a blind man, who, in turn,
heard some woman from a neighboring town singing it, and so the "lineage"
goes. About the word "ralist," he guessed it was "the lonely look on the windows after sunset." If that one word "rayless" can thus take on the greater
meaning implicit in its text, what cannot other words do for a singer! This,
from a lumbering region!

Actually, it is in the lumber camps or among men who formerly worked in
the woods, that some of the rarest ballads, that some of the finest lines and
most picturesquely adapted tunes are recovered. After the day's work "back
in," or on the log drives, men would sit around on benches in the cookhouse,
near the stove, telling yarns and swapping stories in their tunes. I can even
now almost smell the hazy tobacco smoke and the steam of wet socks and
mittens suspended on "Devil's Spiders."**

A song known as "The Shanty Boys" tells all about drying socks and
"lonely hours" whiled away in the lumber woods. In fine fashion, Michael
Barden, now of Massachusetts, sang of what commonly goes on in lumber
camps.

On Elmore Mountain in mid-Vermont in a lumber camp was sung "The

---

* *Vermont Folk Songs and Ballads,* p. 19.
** From the top of a spruce tree, a man would take a cutting which included the complete circle of small twigs; strip them of bark and, while still moist, curl them back to form
from each twig a hook. Then this cutting was hung bottom-side up to form a rack for
drying his socks and mittens. Each man has his own "Devil."

Green Willow Tree,"* "House Carpenter,"** certain murder songs, others of wit and monumental adventures. Elmer George sang nine verses of "Fair Lucy," which was thought to have been extinct in England for a hundred years when Cecil Sharp found it in Manchester, Kentucky.

Considering river drivers in the Katahdin Mountain region, there are ballads handed down from Elizabethan times, ballads beloved of Samuel Pepys, ballads showing many changes and accretions since ships sailed the seven seas and brought cargoes from foreign and fabled lands. We visited Hanford Hayes, seventy-six years old, an ex-foreman of the log drives on the East Branch of the Penobscot. He was living alone, when we found him, trapping bears for their bounty, making axe-helves by hand and, until his eyesight failed, potato picking after the diggers have gone through the fields in September. He sang a fine version of "The Suffolk Miracle," of "Andrew Bardeen," of "Sir James, the Rose." We had written we were coming to see him again. He was ready for us. In the doorway of his shack, he explained, "The rats kept me awake most of the night, so I remembered one song after another." He settled back in his chair, closed his eyes, beat time with one foot, and words stood out "as if sung in the dark." Towards sunset time he led us up into his hill pasture, where sharp against the sky ranged Katahdin and a rim of Western mountains. "That is Traveler," he pointed. "You see it twenty-six miles while you're driving the East Branch. Men called the mountain 'Traveler' because from any point on the stream they could see it and know their direction. That is Mt. Turner with the Wassatoquoit alongside. That is Sugar Loaf with the Sebois running by it." So he named mountain after mountain, always with the stream he visualized at its foot. Over there men had sung among themselves the songs he knew and the songs they knew— songs we were to hear later as we followed addresses given by one lumberman after another, scattered all over northern Maine. We could bring news from one man to another—messages mechanically recorded, such as, "Hello, Linnie, this is Hanford Hayes speaking," etc.

Itinerants have preserved a number of the most valuable ballads in our collection. A scissors grinder, mender of clocks and locks and barker at village fairs sang a fine fragment of "The Factor's Song." Later Miss Olney was to

* *Country Songs of Vermont,* p. 40.
** *Garland of Green Mountain Song,* p. 80.

d in northern Maine fifty-two verses. As far as we know this is the complete
ng. In the "Black Letter Copy" in the British Museum there are forty-seven
rses. There it is known as the "Turkey Factor"—referring to the country, not
e bird. In its earliest known form it is the theme of a Persian legend. . . .

ng by Mr. Michael Barden of 64 Westmorland Street, Dorchester, Massachusetts, as
own among the men in Thetford Mines, Canada.

H. H. F., Collector
February 14, 1946

THE SHANTY BOYS

Lads if you will listen, I'll sing to you a song.
It's all about the lumber men and how they get along.
They're a lot of jolly fellows, so merry and so fine,
They spend the winter pleasantly all cutting down the pine.

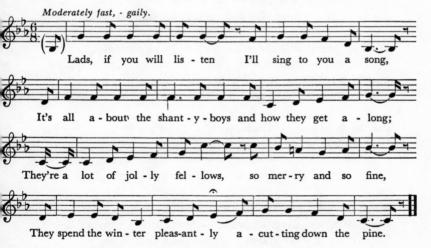

They leave their homes all in the fall, the girls they loved so dear.
Some to their lonesome pine-woods, their passage for to steer.
They leave their homes all in the fall, all winter to remain,
All waiting for spring-time to roll 'round the girls again.

Spring-time will soon roll 'round, and glad will be the day.
Some to their homes and sweethearts, while others will wander away.
Takes farmers, and sailors, likewise mechanics, too,
Takes all sorts of trades-men to form a lumbering crew.

The choppers and the sawyers, they lay their timber low.
The skidders and the yardsmen, will swing them to and fro.
Along comes the teamsters before break of day,
Load up, my boys, two thousand feet. To the river haste away.

Dinner time will soon roll 'round, it will be loudly scream.
Lay down your saws and axes, hurray for pork and beans.
While washing is a-going on, the cook will dinner cry,
To see the men get up and dust for fear they'd lose their pie.

When dinner it is over, out of the camp we'll go.
We'll all load up our pipes and smoke till everything looks blue.
Our foreman he will hollar—"Hurray, my boys, hurray,"
To see them get their caps and mitts to the woods we'll haste away.

We'll all go out with cheerful hearts and well contented minds.
For the wintry winds it never blew cold amongst the weary pine.
You'll hear the saws and axes ring until the sun goes down,
Hurray, my boys, your day's work's done for the shanty we are bound.

For the shanty we are bound with cold and wet feet.
We'll all take off our shoe-packs and supper we will eat.
The cook will hollar "Supper" and we'll all rise up and go;
For it ain't the style for one of the boys to lose their hash, you know.

When supper it is over, shoe-packs are thrown aside.
Caps, mitts, socks, rags and shoe-packs are all hung up and dryed.
At 9 o'clock or there about, into our bunks we'll climb,
To pass away those lonely hours a working in the pine.

About four in the morning, our foreman he'll cry out,
"Hurray, ye roving teamsters, it's time ye were out."

The cook he'll then get up all in a fright and rage,
"Good God, I lost my shoe-pack, my sock is gone astray."

The choppers will then get up, their socks they cannot find.
They will leave it on the teamsters and curse them till they're blind.
They will laugh and joke and carry on to pass away the time;
For a jollier crew you never knew than shanty boys in pine.

Springtime will soon roll 'round, and glad will be the day.
Lay down your saws and axes in haste to break away.
While the floating ice is going and business is alive,
Three hundred able-bodied men a-wanting on the drive.

With pike poles and peavys all woodsmen do go.
To risk their dear lives on the Misquagan River O.
On a cold and frosty morning, all shivering with the cold;
So much ice upon our peavy stocks we can them scarcely hold.

Here is an ending to my song, and I know it to be true.
If there's any of you that doubt it, just inquire of our lumbering crew.
It was in Willie Murphy's shanty that this song was sang with glee.
Here is an ending to my song, and it was composed by me.

East Calais, Vermont, Mr. Elmer George sang this song as learned in his childhood
 me fifty years ago from Mr. Newell Slayton.

H. H. F., Collector
July 30, 1933

FAIR LUCY

(Child 51)

(Repeat last two lines in each verse.)

Fair Lucy was sitting in her own father's hall,
Making her lamency mourn,
When who should come there but her own brother dear,
Saying; "What makes fair Lucy mourn?"

"O I have a cause for to grieve," she said,
"And a reason for to mourn;
For the babe that lies in yon cradle asleep,
Dear Brother, it is your own."

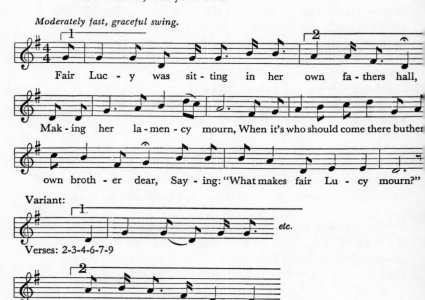

He took her by the lily-white hand
And led her into the woods
And what he done there I never shall disclose
But he spilt fair Lucy's blood.

"O what is that upon your frock,
My son, come tell to me?"
"It is just one drop of fair Lucy's blood
And that you plain can see."

"O what will your father say to you,
My son, come tell to me?"

"I shall step my foot on board of a ship
And my face he never shall see."

"What will you do with your pretty little babe,
My son, come tell to me?"
"I shall leave them here at my father's command
For to keep him company."

"O what will you do with your houses and your lands
My son, come tell to me?"
"I shall leave them here at my father's command
For to set my children free."

"O what will you do with your pretty little wife
My son, come tell to me?"
"She shall step her foot on board of the ship
And sail away with me."

"O when will you return again?
My son, come tell to me."
"When the sun and the moon meet on yonders green hills
And I'm sure that never will be."

nt by Mr. Hanford Hayes of Staceyville, Maine.

H. H. F., Collector
December 30, 1940

THE HOLLAND HANDKERCHIEF

(Child 272)

There was a lord lived in this town;
His praises went the country round.
He had a daughter, a beauty bright
On her he placed his heart's delight.

O, many a lord a-courting came
But none of them could her fancies gain

Till a poor young man of a low degree
Came under hand and she fancied he.

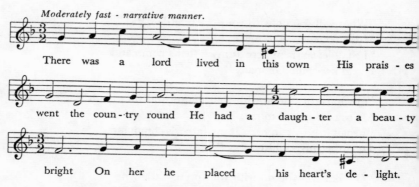

Moderately fast - narrative manner.

There was a lord lived in this town His prais-es
went the coun-try round He had a daugh-ter a beau-ty
bright On her he placed his heart's de-light.

And when her father came this to hear
He separated her far from her dear.
Four scores of miles he had her sent
To her uncle's house at her discontent.

One night as she was for bed bound
And all things ready for to lie down,
She heard the voice of a deadly sound,
Saying, "Oh, loose those bands that so earthy bound."

Her father's steed she quickly knew;
Her mother's mantle and safeguard, too,
And as she mounted on behind,
Rode swifter, faster than the wind.

And all along those words did say,
"My dear and darling, how my head does ache!"
She kissed his lips and those words did say,
"My dear and darling, you're as cold as clay."

Her Holland handkerchief she then pulled out
And bound it 'round his head about,
Saying, "When we get home a good fire we'll have."
But little she knew he came from the grave.

A short while after a little space
They both arrived at her father's gate.
"Un-light, my dear, and go to bed;
You'll find your steed in the stable fed."

But when she entered her father's door,
Her aged father stood on the floor,
Saying, "Father, dear father, did you send for me
By such a messenger, kind sir?" said she.

The hair rose on the old man's head
For he knew quite well her true love was dead.
He wrung his hands and wept full sore
But this young man's darling wept ten times more.

A short while after a little space,
They both arrived at this young man's grave.
Although his body was six weeks dead,
Her Holland handkerchief was 'round his head.

So come all young maidens, a warning take.
Beware, and not your vows to break.
My vows are broke; my true lover gone.
I never can call him back again.

ıg by Mr. Hanford Hayes of Staceyville, Maine, as learned in the woods.

H. H. F. and A. C. B., Collectors
September 22, 1940

SIR JAMES, THE ROSE

(Child 213)

Of all the northern Scottish Chiefs
That live as warlike men,
The bravest was Sir James, the Rose,
A knight of muckle fame.

His growth was like the thrifty fir
That crowns the mountain's brow
And wavering o'er his shoulders broad
Bright locks of yellow flow.

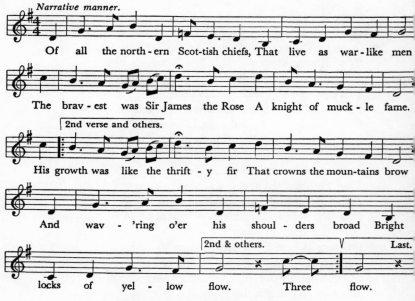

Narrative manner.

Of all the north-ern Scot-tish chiefs, That live as war-like men

The brav-est was Sir James the Rose A knight of muck-le fame.

2nd verse and others.

His growth was like the thrift-y fir That crowns the moun-tains brow

And wav-'ring o'er his shoul-ders broad Bright

2nd & others. / Last.

locks of yel-low flow. Three flow.

Three years he fought on bloody fields
Against their English king.
Scarce two and twenty summers yet
This fearless youth had seen.

It was fair Mathildy that he loved—
That girl with beauty rare—
And Margaret on the Scottish throne
With her could not compare.

Long he had wooed, long she'd refused
It seemed, with scorn and pride
But after all confessed her love;
Her faithful words, denied.

My father was born a cruel lord.
This passion does approve.
He bids me wed Sir John a Grame
And leave the one I love.

My father's will I must fulfill,
Which puts me to a stand.
Some fair maid in her beauty bloom
May bless you with her hand.

"Are those the vows, Mathildy dear,"
Sir James, the Rose did say,
"And would Mathildy wed the Grame
When she's sworn to be my bride?"

"I only spoke to try thy love.
I'll ne'er wed man but thee.
The grave shall be my bridal bed
Ere Grames my husband be.

"You take this kiss, fair youth," she said,
"In witness of my love,
May every plague down on me fall
The day I break my vows."

Ere they had met and there embraced,
Down by a shady grove,
It was on a bank beside a burn
A blooming shelltree stood.

Concealed beneath the undie wood
To hear what they might say,
A brother to Sir John the Grame
And there concealed he lay.

Ere they did part the sun was set.
At haste, he then replied,

"Return, return, you beardless youth,"
He loud insulting cries.

"O it's of my brother's slight love
Rests softly on your arm."
Three paces back the youth retired
To save himself from harm.

Then turned around the beardless youth
And quick his sword he drew
And through his enemy's crashing blows
His sharp-edged weapon drew.

Grame staggered back. He reeled and fell
A lifeless lump of clay.
"So falls my foes," said valliant Rose,
And straightly walked away.

Through the green woods he then did go
Till he reached Lord Bohan's Hall
And at Mathildy's window stood
And thus began to call.

"Art thou asleep, Mathildy dear?
Awake, my love, awake.
Your own true lover calls on you
A long farewell to take.

"For I have slain fair Donald Grame.
His blood is on my sword
And distant are my faithful men.
They can't assist their lord.

"To the Isle of Skye, I must awa'
Where my twa brothers abide.
I'll raise the gallyants of that Isle.
They'll combat on my side."

"Don't do so," the maid replied,
"With me 'til morning stay,
For dark and rainy is the night
And dangerous is the way.

"All night I'll watch you in my park.
My little page I'll send.
He'll run and raise the Rose's clan
Their master to defend."

She laid him down beneath the bush
And rolled him in his plaid.
At a distance stood the weeping maid;
A-weeping for her love.

O'er hills and dales, the page he ran,
Till lonely in the Glen,
'Twas there he met Sir John the Grame
And twenty of his men.

"Where art thou going, my little page?
What tidings dost thou bring?"
"I'm running to raise the Rose's clan
Their master to defend.

"For he has slain fair Donald Grame.
His blood is on his sword,
And distant are his faithful men
They can't assist their lord."

"Tell me where he is, my little page,
And I will thee well reward."
"He sleeps now in Lord Bohan's Hall.
Mathildy, she's his guard."

He spurred his horse at a furious gait
And galloped o'er the lea

Until he reached Lord Bohan's Hall
At the dawning of the day.

Without the gate, Mathildy stood
To whom the Grame replied,
"Saw ye Sir James, the Rose, last night,
Or did he pass this way?"

"Last day at noon fair James, the Rose,
I seen him passing by.
He was mounted on a milk-white steed
And forward fast did fly.

"He's in Edinborotown now by this time
If man and horse proves good."
"Your page now lies who said he was
A-sleeping in the wood."

She wrung her hands and tore her hair
Saying, "Rose, thou art betrayed,
Thou art betrayed all by those means
I was sure you would be saved."

The hero heard a well-known voice;
This valliant knight awoke,
Oh, he awoke and drew his sword
As this brave band appeared.

"So you have slain my brother dear;
His blood as dew did shine
And by the rising of the sun
Your blood shall flow or mine."

"You speak the truth," the youth replies,
"That deeds can prove the man.
Stand by your men and hand to hand
You'll see our valliant stand."

"If boasting words a coward hide,
It is my sword you fear,
It's seen the day on Flodden's Field
When you sneaked in the rear."

"Oh, at him, men, and cut him down!
Oh, cut him down in twain.
Five thousand pounds onto the man
Who leaves him on the plain."

Four of his men—the bravest four—
Fell down before that sword,
But still they scorned that mean revenge
And sought the cowardly Lord.

Till cowardly behind him stole the Grame
And wound him in the side.
Out gushing came his purple gore
And all his garments dyed.

But ne'er of his sword did he quit the grip
Nor fell he to the ground
Till through his enemy's heart his steel
Had pierced a fatal wound.

Grame staggered back. He reeled and fell
A lifeless lump of clay
Whilst down beside him sank the Rose
That fainting, dying lay.

O when Mathildy seen him fall,
"O spare his life," she cried,
"Lord Bohan's daughter begs his life.
She shall not be denied."

The hero heard a well-known voice
And raised his death-closed eyes

And fixed them on the weeping maid,
And faintly this replies,

"In vain, Mathildy, you beg my life.
By death's, it's been denied;
My race is run. Good-bye, my love,"
He closed his eyes and died.

She drew his sword from his left side
With frantic hands, she drew.
"I come, I come, brave Rose," she cried,
"I'm going to follow you."

She leaned the hilt upon the ground
And pressed her snow-white breast;
Laid down upon her lover's face
And endless went to rest.

So come all indulging parents,
By this warning take
And never encourage your children dear
Their sacred vows to break.

As sung by Mr. Nelson Powers of Mattawamkeag, Maine, learned from his father.

M. Olney, Collector
September 20, 1941

THE FACTOR'S SONG

Behold, here's a ditty, the truth and no jest,
Concerning a gentleman lived in the West,
And he by his gaming came to poverty
And afterwards went many voyages to sea.

He being considered a man of great wit,
Three merchants in London, all thinking him fit

For to be their captain and factor also,
A voyage to old Turkey for them he did go.

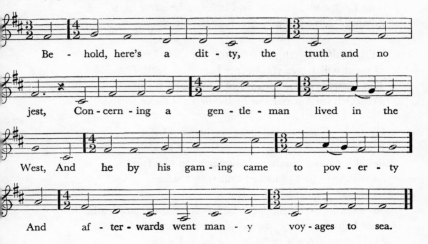

Be - hold, here's   a   dit - ty,   the   truth and   no
jest,   Con - cern - ing   a   gen - tle - man   lived in   the
West, And   he   by   his   gam - ing   came   to   pov - er - ty
And   af - ter - wards went man - y   voy - ages to   sea.

As he was a-travelling in Turkey, he found
A poor man's dead body a-lying on the ground;
He ask-ed the reason and why it there lie
And one of the natives made him this reply.

"This man was a christian, sir, while he drew breath;
His debts being not paid, he must lay above earth."
"O what is the sum then?" the Factor, he cried,
"It's fifty pounds sterling," the old Turk replied.

"This is a large sum," said the Factor, "Indeed,
But to see him lay here, it doth make my heart bleed;"
So by this young Factor the money was paid
And into the grave this dead body was laid.

Then going on along further, he chanced to espy
A beautiful lady just going to die;
A young witty maiden a-strangled must be
For nothing but striking a Turkish lady.

My thoughts on her dying, it filled her with grief
And no one appear-ed unto her relief;
The Factor was grieved and in haste he drew nigh
Saying, "Ain't it a pity this lady should die?

"The fault seemeth small for to take away breath,
O what will I give you to free her from death?"
The answer return-ed was "one hundred pounds,"
To which for her pardon he freelie paid down.

He said, "Honored lady, are we being refrain?
It is be of good comfort, you ne'er shall be slain;
Behold, I have purchased your pardon—be free,
Be willing to go to fair London with me."

She says, "I do thank you who has freed me from death,
I am bound to obey you as long as I've breath,
And if that you please to fair London I'll go
And respect unto you until death I will show."

He carried her over and as it is said,
He set up housekeeping and she was his maid
For to wait upon him, and, finding her just,
The key of his riches he did her entrust.

At length this young Factor was hired once more
For to cross the wide ocean and the billows that roar,
Into a hot country, his course was to steer
To where this girl's father was ruler, we hear.

Then for this hot country this man did prepare;
He bought him fine robes, this country to wear,
He bought him a jacket and I have been told
His servant maid wrought it with silver and gold.

She says, "Dearest master, I do understand
That you are bound Factor unto such a land

And if to the Garland, his court you go in,
I'll pray let this flower-id garment be seen."

He says, "To the Garlander's court I must go,
But the meaning of your words I would like for to know."
She says, "I'll not tell you, the meaning you'll find,"
To which he replied, "I will fulfill your mind."

'Twas in a short time the ship reached her port,
Where straightway he went to the Garlander's court;
As custom prevail-ed so far in that place,
It was usual to give some rich gift to the grace.

The gift was accepted and as he stood by,
On this flower-id garment your prince cast his eye,
Which made him astonished and this he did say,
"Friend, who wrought your garment, come, tell me, I pray?"

"If my grace will admit, I was in Turkey one day,
I espied a young lady just going to die;
I paid for her pardon one hundred pound
And I took her home with me to fair London town.

"Now she is my housekeeper while I'm in this land
And when of my coming she did understand,
She flowered this garment, gave charge unto me
To let it be seen by your great majesty."

Thus said the old prince, "This robe I now wear,
It is of the same flower and spot I declare;
Your maid wrought them both, she is my daughter dear,
I have not heard from her—'Tis now most three years.

" 'Twas out of respect to a neighboring friend,
I sent her on shipboard—I've not seen her since;
I feared that the ocean did prove her sad grave
Till since into Turkey she was taken a slave.

"For the loss of my daughter to whom I thought dead,
Has caused many a tear in this court to be shed;
The princesses, her mother, for her could not rest,
Drew thousands and millions of sighs to her breast.

"Your ship it shall be richly laden, indeed,
I'll send a ship for her convoy with speed;
Since it is so ordered you've saved my child's life,
Bring her alive to me, I'll make her your wife.

"If you should not live for to bring her to me,
The first man that brings her his bride she shall be;
A hundred, a thousand a year she shall have;
It is therefore take care my dear daughter to save!"

The ship it was ladened, the anchor was weighed
And he and his convoy sailed over with speed
To fair London city, then home he did go
For to let this young princess those tidings to know.

He said, "Honored lady, good news I've to tell,
The old prince, your father, and mother is well;
And your London parent this thing have designed
That in bans of wedlock we both shall be joined.

"Suppose, noble lady, you would not be free
For to marry a poor man, especially me?"
"If you was a beggar, I would be your wife,
When I was near dying you sav-ed my life.

"Come, sell off your goods that you now have in store,
Give all of your money to those who are poor
And let us be going with speed o'er the main,
For I long to be home,—my dear parents again."

On this was dispatched and as they sailed away
In the ship that her father sent for her convoy;

But mark what was acted on the ocean wide,
To deprive this young Factor of his royal bride.

The captain conveyed them with speed o'er the deep.
One night as the Factor, he lay in his sleep;
To fulfill his promise, him overboard cast
Saying, "Now I shall gain this fair lady at last."

There happened to be a small island at hand,
To where he did swim as we do understand;
So now we will leave him awhile for to mourn
And unto the ship we'll return back again.

'Twas early next mourning when daylight did peep,
They awoke this young lady out of her sleep,
Saying, "Honored young lady, the Factor's not here,
He fell overboard and is drowned, we fear."

Then into deep mourning she instant-lie went,
For the loss of her lover, sad tears to lament.
"Since there's no one can help it, your weeping refrain,
Behold! you shall see your dear parents again."

Then in a short time the ship reached the port,
Where this lady went weeping to her poor father's court
And she was received with great joy and great mirth,
Saying, "Where is the young man that has saved you from death?"

The captain replied, "As he lay in his sleep,
He fell overboard and was drowned in the deep;
Your grace said the man who should bring your child home
Should have her for a wife, sir. For that I have come."

"Yes, that was my promise," the old prince, he cried,
"What sayest thou, daughter, wilt thou be his bride?"
"O yes, honored father, O yes, if you please,
But for him saved my life I will mourn forty days."

On this desolate island the Factor, he lay
In the flood of tears weeping two nights and a day,
Till on the wide ocean appeared in his view
A little old man paddling a canoe.

The Factor hailed to him and bade him to stay,
The old man drew nigh and this he did say,
"Friend, how came thou hither, I pray let me know?"
So he told him the matter and where he would go.

"Now," said the old man, "If it's here you do lie,
It is with grief and hunger—in short time you'll die;
O what will you give me?" the old man he cried,
"I have nothing to give you," the Factor replied.

"Now," said the old man, "Here is one thing I'll do,
Give me the first babe that is born unto you,
When it doth arrive at full thirty months old
And you shall be conveyed to the place you have told."

The Factor considered this thing would cause grief
And also without it there was no relief;
He cried, "Life is sweet, and my life for to save,
Take me to the place and your will you shall have."

The Factor's conveyed there, to his great joy,
Where the lady was weeping for the loss of her love;
Looking out of the window, beholding him there,
It was joy from great weeping, transported she were.

He entered the gate and with great joy was received.
This lady she met him, who for him was grieved,
She cried, "O my darling, my joy and my dear!
Where have you long tarried, I pray let me hear?"

"Where I have long tarried, I now will relate,
Since I have arriv-ed at your father's gate.

I was cast overboard as I lay in my sleep,
I think 'twas the captain threw me in the deep."

'Twas then the ship captain was sent for in speed,
On hearing the Factor had came there, indeed;
He proved himself guilty like a cruel knave,
Leaped into the ocean which proved his sad grave.

Next day the old prince for to fulfill his mind,
The lady and Factor in wedlock was jined;
Within the compass and space of three years,
They had a fine son and a daughter, we hear.

The first was a son and a perfect beauty
And was well beloved by the whole family;
In full thirty months the old man came for his child
That carried the Factor from this desert Isle.

'Twas with a grim look the old man did appear,
Which made the court shudder and trouble with fear;
"O what shall we do for it's sure he's no man.
He will have our darling, do all that we can."

"O yes," said the old man, "I will have my due,
Here is one babe for me and another for you,
O yes, I will have him, come, give him to me!"
To which the whole family wept bitterly.

They first having kissed it and down the tears fell,
Then they did embrace it and bade it farewell;
She says, "For the sake of my husband and I,
I part with my first born, but, for it I die."

'Twas with a grim look the old man he did say,
"Sir, don't you remember in Turkey one day
You spied a dead body lying on the ground
And to have it buried you paid fifty pound?

"Now I am the spirit of that poor body,
I saved you for that Christian act unto me;
So you may keep your child and may God bless you all!"
And away then he vanishes out of the hall.

Having gone, the old prince and princess likewise
And the babe's tender parents with tears in their eyes,
They first having kissed it, their darling, their son,
Saying, "Child, hadst thou left us, we would be undone."

So leaving the court full of joy and great mirth,
For to love one another while God giveth breath;
So by this young Factor you can see indeed,
No mortal can alter what God has decreed.*

. . . People who preserve ballads from generation to generation are likely to
show just as much critical sense in the ways they develop a narrative quality
in the tunes as in the words. They are, with the airs, unrestricted by the gram-
matical conventions of the written word or of music. It is puzzling to explain
the several tunes we have recorded which have been handed down with archaic
intervals. There are a few ballads sung by persons who can carry a tune when
the tradition is of melodies *on* pitch, but who, in certain songs, intentionally
sing slightly off-pitch. The narrative effect of the air is vastly enhanced by this
manner. Were such off-pitches passed on orally by singers with inaccurate
hearing and no sense of pitch, or are these tunes survivals of pre-instrumental
days? Just as we have many airs determined by the gap scales of certain
instruments, why should we not have some airs determined by a folk-choice
when there was no grammar of music? These widened and lessened intervals
seem quite in nature when used by a singer who has not been brought up on
the diatonic scale and harmonies such as Bach developed on the "well-
tempered clavichord." They have a character all their own. Certain singers
notably the Irish, embellish a tune with grace notes, turns, and willful aber-
rations of pitches, thus producing a most haunting beauty. The singer but
knows that he suits the tune to the words. He may have a five-line stanza in
a ballad, or six lines before the beginning of the usual quatrain. These h

---

* Last four words spoken.

apts by repetitions in his tunes which emphasize consummately the vivid
es. He has his own aesthetic satisfactions.

Many airs have a striking resemblance to the so-called Ecclesiastical modes
the canto-fermo of the Roman Church Service.

Possibly the music of early Christians, though determined by modes of
inged instruments, harked back to the fixed intervals of the syrinx. Later,
: habits of musical thought may have come from the sanctuary or from the
urch porch into the street. Certainly it is in these same intervals that we
w find old ballads of romances, conquests, tragedies, robberies, etc.
scendants of ancient Grecian ecclesiastical modes have entered the folk
1es of many peoples. The Scandinavians, the Celts, the Gaels took them
er; they suited themselves in the way they used them. Certainly there seems
be in Mr. Degreenia's tune to Mary Alling, (a variant of one for the same
llad current in the times of Charles II) a reappearance of the air to "the
ckoo," a song I recorded in the Gaelic as learned by ear by Mrs. James
acNiel now of Barrie, Ontario. Her parents brought the ancient words in
is tune from the Isle of Barra, Outer Hebrides, to Nova Scotia. Though they
ve them their own varying characteristics, the latest generations of these
elodies still bear a family resemblance.

Cuathiciag Ghorm

"The Cuckoo" translated from the Gaelic by the singer runs:

> O hail to thee, sweet cuckoo,
> With your sweetest refrain
> The music of your voice reaching thru the woods
> Brings lightness to our hearts.
>
> How she would love to hear in the morning
> The bird on the highest tree branch
> And with night coming, still there
> With the falling of the dew!

There are occasional apt folk choices of inspired rhythm and tempos en-
ancing the narration of the song. Particularly is this true in "The Banks of
ow Lee" as sung by Mr. Edward Forbes, of the Fogg Museum in Cambridge,

Massachusetts. Were he to sing the lines in any other tempo than as traditio
ally known to him, the sense of flowing waters would not be a natural pa
of the arch-dialogue. As in the popular song, "Old Man River" the origin
tempo carries the resistless, unhurried sweep of the Mississippi. Alter it ev
so slightly, speed or slacken its progress and there is no accompanying riv
The same is true of Mr. Forbes' "clear, purling stream." That is why
metronome mark is vitally important to give the complete effect to the lea
imaginative reader. . . .

Sung by Mr. Edward Forbes, Director of the Fogg Museum, Cambridge, Massachuset
as learned in the early nineties from a friend.

H. H. F., Collect
December 31, 194

THE BANKS OF LOW LEE

"Good morrow, good morrow, good morrow," said she,
"O, where are you going, fair lady?" said he.
"I'm going to the banks, to the banks of Low Lee
For to see the waters gliding, hear the nightingale sing;
For to see the waters gliding, hear the nightingale sing."

Then onward and onward and onward they go
Till they come to the banks, to the banks of Low Lee
And they sit themselves down by a clear purling stream
For to see the waters gliding, hear the nightingale sing;
For to see the waters gliding, hear the nightingale sing."

Then out of his budget a fiddle he drew.
"O pray," said the lady, "pray play me a tune."
And he played her a tune, made the valley to ring.
"Hark, hark!" said the lady, "hear the nightingale sing;
Hark, hark!" said the lady, "hear the nightingale sing!"

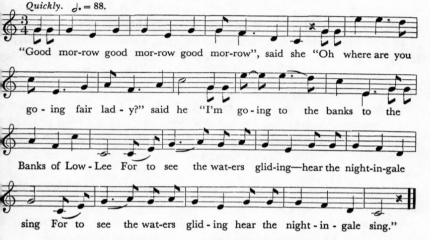

Quickly. ♩. = 88.

"Good mor-row good mor-row good mor-row", said she "Oh where are you go-ing fair lad-y?" said he "I'm go-ing to the banks to the Banks of Low-Lee For to see the wat-ers glid-ing—hear the night-in-gale sing For to see the wat-ers glid-ing hear the night-in-gale sing."

"And now," said the soldier, " 'tis time to give o'er."
"O no," said the lady, "pray play one tune more
For I'd rather hear music to the tune of one string
Than to see the waters gliding, hear the nightingale sing;
Than to see waters gliding, hear the nightingale sing!"

And then said the soldier, "Will you marry me?"
"O no," said the lady, "that never can be.
I've a husband in the Northland with children twice three
And another in the army's too many for me;
And another in the army's too many for me!"

"So I'll go to the Northland, that land of good cheer
And deep in melancholy drink ale, wine and beer
And when I return it will be in the Spring
For to see the waters gliding, hear the nightingale sing;
For to see the waters gliding, hear the nightingale sing!"

. . . In our collection there are many variants of common folk tunes. We ha
a dictaphone record of "The Bailiff's Daughter of Islington," which I c
lected in the early 30's from Mrs. Elwin Burditt. More recently she re-record
the same ballad, but with a tune which much better conveys the story. T
version can be found on page 61 of *The New Green Mountain Songs*
and also on the long-playing record issued by Middlebury College.
Bridgewater, Vermont, an old resident sang of a boy killed by a falling tr
in pioneer days in Hartford. Next we came upon a form of that tune, adapt
to a song known to a singer near Montpelier, where the English lady, in lo
with the man who loved her serving maid, took the maid on a voyage
"plunge her body in the deep." A few weeks later, it cropped up in Grotc
Vermont, as "The Murder of John Dugar"—Irish to the core—a variant
that same tune. Another tune popular in New England has been adapted
the words of "The Drowning Lady" (Rhode Island version), "Kathlee
(Vermont)* and "The Devil's Courtship" (Vermont again). Tunes do g
about.

So do texts. There is a popular hanging-description in a song called "Full
and Warren." We find it is orally known in three different tunes, but eac
tune bears characteristics common to its distribution, be it Irish, English,
Scottish. The Irish singer has a habit of dwelling arbitrarily upon certa
notes, in pauses more common to story-telling than to singing. He uses casu
pitches, grace notes, and turns. Can this ornamentation, sometimes found
Irish singing tradition, be related to the scrolls and arabesques of ancie
Irish art? Even this added question arises: Are there innate characteristics
a nation which show themselves in every form of its art?

The English have a more forthright presentation of their songs. A burdu
common to the older ones is "Down, Down, Down Derry Down"—rath
conclusively expressed. Scottish, English, and Irish texts show objectivity
observation; German texts show more uniformly a subjectivity of expressio
That is, in British texts it is likely to be the thing itself that is tragic; in th
German texts it is likely to be the sentimentalizing that makes its poignar
appeal to the emotions.

---

* *The New Green Mountain Songster,* p. 41.

This song was sung by Edward Horton, a half-breed Indian in Plymouth Union, Vermont, who learned it years ago from Stillman Maxham of Bridgewater, Vermont. He called it:

H. H. F., Collector
Early 1930's

BOY KILLED BY A FALLING TREE IN HARTFORD

Come, all you young people far and near,
A true relation you shall hear
Of a young man as ere you see
Was killed in Hartford by a tree.

Come all young peo-ple far and near, A true re-
la-tion you shall hear, Of a young man as
ere you see Was killed in Hart-ford by a tree.

Variants:
Verse 3:

Near fort-y rods to an ash tree The top was
dry as you may see. He

Verse 8:

Oh, 'twas an aw-ful sight to see. So fair and
spright-ly youth was he All

One Isaac Alcutt was his name,
Who lately into Hartford came,
Residing with his brother James,
Last Thursday noon went, as it seems,

To cut some timber for a sled,
The snow being deep, he had to wade
Near forty rods to an ash tree—
The top was dry as you may see.
He cut the tree off the stump;
The top being dry, threw back a clump,

It fell and struck him on the head,
And smote him down; yet was not dead.
There this poor sufferer senseless lay
All the remainder of that day.

His charming face plunged in the snow,
And from his head the blood did flow.
His friends and neighbors being gone,
Not knowing that he had withdrawn,

No search was made by anyone
Until the setting of the sun.
Then Mr. Daniels and his son
Alarmed, set out on the run;

They soon beheld him with surprise,
And gazed on him with steadfast eyes.
They first supposed him to be dead
Till by some motion of his head

They found that life was in him left;
He moved his head, drawing his breath.
Oh, 'twas an awful sight to see
So fair and sprightly youth was he
All coiled and crippled in a heap;
'Twould cause the stoutest heart to weep.

One of his hands was stiffly froze,
Part of his arms, some of his toes,
The blood had issued from his wound
And thawed a passage to the ground.

They took him up and bore him home,
Put him to bed in a warm room.
They rubbed his limbs and dressed his wounds
And strove to force some cordial down.

But all in vain, the passage choke;
His blood was chilled, his skull was broke.
All useful medicines were applied,
But he on that same evening died.

The heavy news did soon arrive
To his dear friends and relatives,
It filled their hearts with bitter grief,
But he was past all their relief.

When all his friends had gathered round,
A sermon preached by Elder Brown,
His pleasant corpse was borne away
To mingle with its native clay.

He was but twenty years of age
And some odd months, as we are alleged;
He was both virtuous, fair and kind,
Beloved by every civil mind.

Think on his virtuous, weeping friends,
Mourn not for him, but for your sins,
For sin is the procuring cause
That brings God's judgment unawares.

Let this a warning be to all
To be prepared when God shall call.
Methinks I hear his voice aloud
Saying, "Prepare to meet your God."

Sent by Mr. Elmer George of East Calais, Vermont. As sung by his grandfather, Ches
Chase.

H. H. F., Collec
December 27, 19

THE LADY AND THE FARMER'S SON

Young lovers all, I pray draw near
And a relation you shall hear
Of how a lady was undone
By loving of a farmer's son.

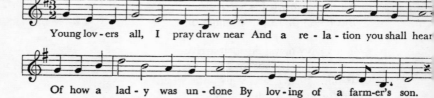

His age, it was just twenty-two
As I the truth do tell to you.
He was well formed in every limb.
This lady fell in love with him.

She wrote him letters every day,
But he to her would nothing say
Because he knew he was going to wed
Sally, her handsome chamber-maid.

As she was walking in the grove,
By chance she met with her own true love,
Saying, "Kind sir, upon my life
I do intend to be your wife."

"O lady fair, that cannot be—
For you to be a wife to me,
Because you know I am engaged
To Sally, your handsome chamber-maid."

She wrung her hands and tore her hair,
And cried, "Alas I'm in despair.
How can you slight me so?" she said,
"All for a silly chambermaid?"

"If only I was from her free
Then I could love you tenderly,
But I am bound to her by oath,
You know I cannot wed you both."

The lady thought, "If that be so,
I soon will prove her overthrow,
For she my waiting maid shall be
And we will cross the raging sea."

This lady had contrived it so
All for to work her overthrow—
As this poor maiden lay asleep
She plunged her body in the deep.

Now this fair lady on return
Found conscience like vexatious burn
For never could she be at rest
Until the deed she had confessed.

'Tis now she lies confined in jail.
The Lord have mercy on her soul.
Distracted did this young man run,
In Bedlam lies the farmer's son.

'Twas by the help of curs-ed gold,
This pretty maiden's life was sold.
'Tis now a lass and you may see
Has proved the ruin of all three.

As sung by Mr. W. B. Morton of Groton, Vermont. Mr. Morton was a native of Shelburne, Nova Scotia, one of ten children in a family of Scottish descent. He is now 73 years old. Mr. Morton was told that this murder happened in Digby, Nova Scotia.

H. H. F., Collector
October 19, 1937

THE MURDER OF JOHN DUGAR

Come now, my friends, both old and young;
Give your attention, ev'ry one.
This murdrous deed rings everywhere
That happened in the County Clare.

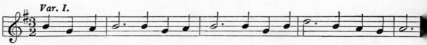

Come now my friends, both old and young; Give your at - ten - tion, ev -'ry one

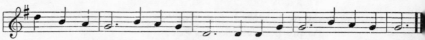

This mur-drous deed rings ev -'ry - where, That hap-pened in the Coun-ty Claire.

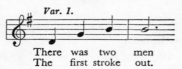

There was two men
The first stroke out.

There was two men in County Clare
Proved their shipmates for many a year;
At last a difference came to sight
That showed they could no more unite.

The first broke out was John Dugar.
In his own hands he took the law.
He throwed off coat and hat with might
And dared the other out to fight.

The other being Charles Robbisher
Who would not fight with John Dugar
And of those words was heard to him say,
If he was hung for it next day.

He went at Captain Charles as well.
How stilly lying, no tongue can tell,
When Charles for water made a start,
He plunged a dagger to his heart.

When Captain Charles did reach his house,
So badly bleeding at the mouth
And also bleeding at the side,
And so remained until he died.

Then from the shore John took a boat
And round to Weymouth he did float.
So calmly did the murderer show,
Then took the woods for Liverpool.

From Liverpool he then did ship
And for G'ocester took a trip.
Detective Hut did on him rail
And for the deed put him in jail.

Into his lonely cellar-room
He waits his trial—and that's in June—
To stand a chance, which soon will be
To be condemned or else set free.

At last his trial does appear
And from the gallows he is clear.
If from the laws of man he's clear,
Before his God he must appear.

Ye blooming youths, ye that have saw
The fearful state of John Dugar,
Take caution by this awful state
For you see what follows when it's too late.

As sung by Mr. Charles Finnemore of Bridgewater, Maine.

H. H. F., Collect
September 24, 19

FULLER AND WARREN

Ye sons of Columbia, attention now I call
To a story I'm about for to tell
Which happened of late in the Indiana State
By a hero there was none could excel.

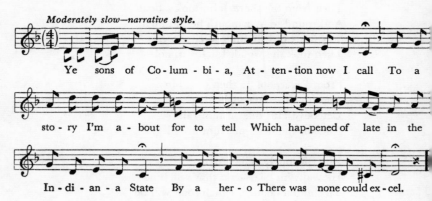

Moderately slow—narrative style.

Ye sons of Co - lum - bi - a, At - ten - tion now I call To a
sto - ry I'm a - bout for to tell Which hap-pened of late in the
In - di - an - a State By a her - o There was none could ex - cel.

Like Samson he courted the fairest of the sex
Intending to make her his bride
But like young Delilah fair, O she did his heart ensnare
And she robbed him of his honor and his pride.

When Fuller came to hear he was deprived of his dear
How she promised by the powers to wed,
To Warren he did go with his heart full of woe
And those words unto Warren he said.

"Now, Warren, you have wronged me for to gratify your cause
By reporting I've left a prudent wife,
Now adknowledge you've wronged me, or I will break the law,
Warren, I'll deprive you of your life."

Then Warren he replied, "Your request must be denied
For my heart unto your darling is bound.
Furthermore, let me say that this is our wedding day
In spite of all your heroes of this town."

Then Fuller in a passion of love and anger flew
And then he began for to cry.
With one fatal shot he killed Warren on the spot
Then smiling says, "I'm ready now to die."

Then Fuller he was taken by the honorable board
By the laurel of Auburn to die
Such an ignominious death for to swing above the earth
Like Homer on the gallows so high.

Now the time was drawing nigh when poor Fuller he had to die.
To his friends he bid them all adieu;
On the gallows he did stand and he was a handsome man.
On his breast he wore a ribbon of blue.

Ten thousand spectators they smote upon their breast
And the guards they dropped tears from their eyes
Saying, "Curs-ed was she—she has caused his misery
And she ought to in his stead have to die."

Come all you young married men who has got a prudent wife,
Be loving, be true and be kind.
You may look in the book of Moses, of Genises, and Job
And the truth of my story you'll find.

For love it is a lottery and he who wins the prize.
She may be pleasing to his mind and his eyes
But the man that never marries is the man that's counted wise
So ladies and gentlemen "Good-bye."

. Folk idiom, choice of tonalities, re-used tunes, riddles, new ballads com-
unded of lines from different ancient ballads, and themes common to dif-

ferent peoples and countries, all throw a strong light upon ways of nativ
thought and upon periods. The latter-day appearance of this literature an
music is still richly redolent of its separate or communal meaning. Even mor
its effect is discovered infrequently in the ordinary speech of a singer. To ci
an instance: We talked with a man in Calais, Vermont, who spoke of
schoolmaster as one deserving "three dips in the river"—a phrase whic
occurs in a song which ridiculed "Old Hewson, the Cobler."* Hewson, on
a cobbler, was a General in Cromwell's Army. More than that, he was a judg
who signed the death warrant of Charles the First. The folk-notion of his ju
deserts had been perpetuated ever since in the line "three dips in the river
So I asked the Vermont singer if he knew the song about

> "I gave him three dips in the river,
> And so fondly bade him goodnight."

He recalled hearing it years before but had never learned it all. Yet he had
a commonplace in his everyday speech the "three dips in the river."
When sung by Mrs. Lily Delorme, in Cadyville, New York, the cobbler w
"Hobson." Her version came from her forebears in Starksboro, Vermont.

Sung by Mrs. Lily Delorme of Cadyville, New York.
M. Olney, Marjorie Porter, Collect
August 16, 1943

HOBSON, THE COBBLER

My name is Jack Hobson the cobbler.
I serv-ed my time out in Kent.
They called me an old fornicator
Before I had time to repent.

REFRAIN:

With me twing, ing, ing,
     ming, ing, ing, yawdy.
Me twinging-ing
     minging-ing

---

* Published, with tune, in *The New Green Mountain Songster*, p. 223.

With a roo, boo, boo,
  boo, boo, boo, bawdee.
fol-de-dee-daw di-day.

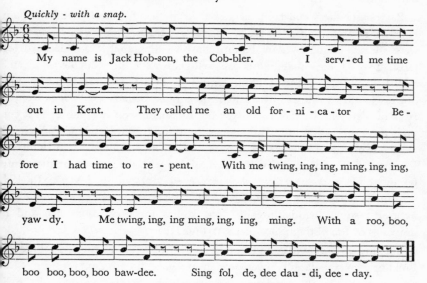

Quickly - with a snap.

My name is Jack Hob-son, the Cob-bler. I serv-ed me time

out in Kent. They called me an old for-ni-ca-tor Be-

fore I had time to re-pent. With me twing, ing, ing, ming, ing, ing,

yaw-dy. Me twing, ing, ing ming, ing, ing, ming. With a roo, boo,

boo boo, boo, boo baw-dee. Sing fol, de, dee dau-di, dee-day.

For seven long years I was a-roving,
The happiest days of my life,
And many's a misfortune I had in.
I got myself hitched to a wife.

My wife she was humpy and dumpy.
O Lord, she was ugly and black
And when I came in to my dinner
She gave me the devil's gin-whack.

But now my troubles are ended,
Since I put an end to her life.
I gave her three dips in the river
And kindly I bade her "good-night."

Why did not such songs as "Little Brown Jug," "Old Black Joe," "John
own's Body," and like popular songs crowd out the older ones? It may be

because there is a ballad state of mind, a ballad appetite, a ballad habit of thought. This lineage of predilection is likely to persist, despite radios, movies and television.

Pioneer scholarly collectors of the ballad in New England were Mrs. Fanny Hardy Eckstorm and Miss Mary Winslow Smythe of Brewer, Maine. They were shortly joined by Mr. Phillips Barry, ballad-analyst and learned folk lorist. Those three collaborators are well-known for the valuable publication *British Ballads from Maine* (Yale University Press). In Vermont, Mrs. Edith Sturgis found in one family enough memorable ballads for "Songs from the Hills of Vermont." More recently, Mrs. Eloise Linscott has published a comprehensive collection of "Folk Songs from Old New England." From the twenty-two-year old collection now at Middlebury College,* in Middlebury, Vermont, four books have been edited, giving with their tunes the most entertaining ballads recovered in the first seven years of field work. In 1941 "Vermont Chap Book" added certain lively texts, no tunes, that made up a natural Sesquicentennial presentation. It has for illustrations pen and ink drawings by the distinguished artist, Arthur Healy.

But any balladmonger had best visit the collection at the Carr Fine Arts Building, for the larger experience in versions, broadsides, recordings, and reminiscences. To the scholar of the English and Scottish versions of the 305 ballads from the valuable collection of the late Professor Francis James Child, can be shown certain Irish findings of several of the same numbers.

Faded manuscripts, many of which have been photographed, show what songs were current in Vermont after the Revolution, and offer comparisons of regional changes. We have verses handwritten on rag paper in early 1800 found by the late Walter Jones in an old drawer in Waitsfield; we have manuscript copybook of about the same period secured in Panton, on Lake Champlain, by the late Charles Tuttle, famous bibliophile of Rutland. Mr. Charles Pratt of Putney, Vermont, presented us with a copious notebook containing songs treasured for four generations of the Cox family in Bradford. In Windsor, with dates 1826 and 1830, exists a book filled with songs penned

---

* At Middlebury College, Middlebury, Vermont, are texts and tunes to all ballads recorded from memories exactly as sung, and fiddle-tunes, call dances, fife-tunes—folk-music generally, making up an index of some eight thousand items. This is known as the Helen Hartness Flanders Collection, but anyone can easily note that it is made up by all the generous contributors she has met. At Middlebury, the ballad itself is teaching the ballad.

by Catherine Amelia Morgan (born 1815) during her childhood. A fifth and larger compilation is *The Green Mountain Songster,* in possession of Mr. Harold Rugg, Assistant Librarian at Dartmouth College. Here are printed, by "an ex-Revolutionary Soldier" at Sandgate, in 1823, "songs to cheer the drooping mind." They prove to be edifying, patriotic, romantic or in a few cases just plain bawdy.

There is occasionally a song of exceptional interest. For instance, in the Morgan manuscript occurs "The White Headed Boy." The year Catherine Morgan was born there was published in "Brattleborough, Vermont for the Book-Sellers" the *Songster's Companion.* On page 19 appears the title "Cupid Benighted," which turns out to be "The White Headed Boy."* Catherine Morgan's version is clearly of folk-transmission. But surely they both hark back to Ode 3 by Anacreon. I noted a resemblance when reading a translation by the Earl of Derby of the Iliad of Homer, to which are appended "Poems Ancient and Modern." Anacreon was a native of Teos, in Ionian Asia Minor, born supposedly 560 years before Christ. Is it not amazing to discover that ode, centuries later and miles apart in folk versions in Vermont? No, because the life history of any folk song or ballad is a continued story.

In the Hay Memorial Library of Brown University, Providence, Rhode Island, is the "Panton" manuscript. It was handwritten supposedly by the Elder Grandey, who left his native Canaan, Connecticut (now Ashley Falls, Massachusetts), to settle in the wilderness of northern Vermont. How this pioneer happened to know "Night in the Green," which he painstakingly set down as he knew it by ear, is a mystery. . . .

---

* Also found in *The American Songster,* Danville, Vermont, 1815, p. 16.

Loaned to H. H. F., July 3, 1951, by the Ascutney Chapter of the DAR in Windsor
Vermont, this hand-penned copybook has a date "1830." There is a half-page of account
with dates of 1826. This book was given the DAR by Adgelon K. Hall (born Nov. 26
1855; died March 10, 1943) "as written by his mother when a girl." One page ha
"Sarah Curtis, James S. Morgan, Alfred, Miss Catherine Amelia Morgan (and) the nam
has changed since this book was composed Mrs. Catherine Amelia P. Hall." This las
is the name of the donor's mother. She was born June 16, 1815 and died October 15
1869. Married August 26, 1833 she lived the rest of her days in Windsor. Copied literatim
et punctatim.

H. H. F., Collecto
July 3, 1951

THE WHITE-HEADED BOY

In the dead of the night
When labours was at rest
All mortals enjoyed
The sweet blefsingf of rest

A boy rapt at my door
And I woke with the nois
Who is there
My rest to distroy

He answered so sofly
So gently and mild
I am a poor little
Unfortunate child

It is a cold rainy night
And I am wet to my skin
My way I have lost
So pray let me in

I opened the door a boy met my sight
He had wings at his shoulders
And rain from them dript
With bows and with arrows the boy was equipt

I stirred up the fire
And sit him down by the side
And with a warm napkin
The wet from him dried

No sooner from wet
And cold he found ease
He takes up his bow
Says away am I if I please

My bow 'tis undamaged
And so is my dart
But you will find trouble
In bearing the smart

                              farewell

rom the translation of the Earl of Derby as published in Vol. II of *"The Iliad of
omer"*.

                                                    H. H. F.

ODE THREE BY ANACREON

At the hour of deep midnight,
When the star of Arctos bright
Wheels beneath Boötes' hand;
And, throughout the drowsy land,
Sleep its gentle influence sheds
On o'er wearied mortals' heads;
Cupid stood my gate before,
Knocking at the bolted door.
"Who," I cried, "is he who shakes
Thus my door—my slumber breaks?"
"Open quick, be not afraid,
'Tis a Child that knocks," he said:
"In the moonless night astray,
Wet and cold, I've lost my way."

I with pity heard, and straight
Lit my lamp, unbarred my gate;
And a Child indeed was there,
Who a bow and quiver bare.
By my hearth I made him stand;
Chafed with mine each icy hand,
Wringing from his hair the rain.
Soon restored to warmth again,
"Come," he said, "I fain would know
If the wet have marred my bow."
Straight he aimed, and through my heart
Shot, as 'twere a gadfly's smart.
Up then leaped the laughing Boy;
"Host," he chuckled, "share my joy;
All uninjured is my bow,
As by proof thy heart shall know."

On February 7, 1952, Miss Marguerite Olney wrote: *"The White Headed Boy* is in *T*
Songster's Companion (1815), on page 19 under the title *'Cupid Benighted'* with s
four-line stanzas as follows:"

M. Olney, Collect

In the dead of the night, when with labor oppress'd
All mortals enjoy the sweet blessings of rest;
Cupid knock'd at my door, I awoke with the noise,
Who is it, I cries, that my rest thus destroys;

He answer'd so softly, so gently and mild,
I am a poor little unfortunate child;
It's a cold rainy night, and I'm wet to the skin,
For I have lost my way, so pray let me in.

In compassion I rose, and striking a light,
I open'd the door, and a boy stood in sight;
He had wings on each shoulder, the rain from him dripp'd,
And with a bow and arrow he was equipp'd.

I stir'd up my fire and sat down by his side,
And with a warm napkin the rain from him dry'd;
I chaff'd him all o'er to keep out the cold air,
And I wrung with my hands the wet out of his hair.

No sooner from wet and from cold he got ease,
Than, taking his bow, he said, mam if you please;
If you please, I would fain by experience know,
If the rain has not damag'd the string of my bow.

Then straight from his quiver an arrow he drew,
Which he aim'd at my heart, and twang went the yew;
My bow is not damag'd nor yet is my dart,
But you'll find some trouble in bearing the smart.

. The original source of its theme may be *Pecorone,* by Sir Giovanni Fioren-
o, printed in Italy in 1544. Shakespeare uses the situation in *"The Merchant*
Venice" known to be in existence as a play in 1598, though not printed
fore 1600. Strange to come upon it on the shores of Lake Champlain with
o more verses than are in a broadside form in the Folger Shakespeare
emorial Library in Washington! This pioneer in the frontier outpost knew
more verses of the ballad than were printed in Buchan's "Gleanings of
otch, English and Irish Scarce Old Ballads," Peterhead, 1825.

In quoting "The Night in Green," I cannot surely attribute its American
tribution to Vermont, because the Elder Grandey may have learned in his
tive town of Canaan, Connecticut, the songs he penned during his lifetime
Vermont. This 18th century manuscript of 132 pages is interesting as
gards both British and early American ballads. "The Wife of Auchter-
uchty" illustrates a Scottish text. English songs current during the Revolu-
n like "Ye Parliament of England" show intense feeling. An Americanized
xt of the latter was sent me by James Copeland of Bridgeport, Connecticut.
quote both for comparisons.

In search for present-day members of the Grandey lineage I was in Ashley
lls, Massachusetts, formerly Canaan, Connecticut. No luck! Well then,
aat other addresses should be consulted? The trail led me down a long hill,
ep as the cascade falling down through the trees beside us. At the foot was

the village of West Cornwall, and the Housatonic River flowing under a long covered bridge. I found a house beside the river at a turn in the road where lived a correspondent, Mr. Oscar Degreenia. He was leaning back against the house in a Windsor chair, quite as if the sound of the stream were flowing steadily through him. I introduced myself, telling him I'd like to live within the sound of a river. "You'd git tired of it," he remarked succinctly. He remembered having written me of songs he knew; so he took me into the house. Shortly he was singing to me "Daily Growing" and a form of "Barbara Allen" he knew as "Mary Alling." He gave also his version of "Lord Randall" where the lover admits he was fed a poisonous snake instead of the usual "eels fried in butter."

He sang "The Three Brothers" until the sea fight of robbers in the times of Henry VII was fairly in the room with us, lit with Connecticut sunlight.

We have another sea fight of this doughty period as sung in Maine by Mr. Alonzo Lewis of the Agamenticus section. The Englishman, Captain John Ward, while in command of one of the King's ships, persuaded the crew to become pirates. Between 1604 and 1609 they chased and robbed whatever French and Spanish ships they encountered. One of Drake's ships, the Rainbow, finally gave them battle and ended their "robbing all on the high sea."

To return to the front parlor and Mr. Degreenia's singing, there was a pause for recalling a certain ballad. His granddaughter at a nearby piano fingered the tune of "Come Thou Font of Every Blessing"—much to my anxiety. How could he remember any other song with that hymn tune in his ears? . . .

Copied literatim et punctatim from the Grandey Blankbook, loaned to H. H. F. by the late Mr. Charles Tuttle. The old English long "s" is represented by an "f."

H. H. F., Collector
February 13, 1939

NIGHT IN GREEN

A northern Lord of high renown
Two daughters had the elder brown
The younger beautiful and fare
A noble knight came riding there

Their Father said kind sir I have
Two daughters here which do you crave
She that is beautiful he cry'd
The noble Lord he then Reply'd

She's charming beautiful & gay
And is not to be given away
But as rich jewels bought & sold
She shall fetch me her weight in gold

The price I think you need not grutch
For I shall freely give as much
To her bron sister if I can
Light on some loving gentleman

With that reply'd the noble knight
I'd rather have the Beauty bright
At your own price renowned lord
Than tother with that large reward

The bargain being fairly made
Before the money could be paid
He borrow'd of a wealthy Jew
The mighty sun and writings drew

That if he mist or faild a day
As many ounces as she should weigh
Of his own flesh instead of Gold
As agreed there the money told

Then he Return'd Immediately
To the great lord where he did buy
His daughter beautiful and fair
And paid him down the money there

He bought her then it was well known
To all mankind she was his own

By her a Son he did enjoy
A sweet and handsome sprightly boy

At length the time of pay drew near
And therefore he began to fear
The torter of the crewel Jew
Because the money it was due

And since the same he could not pay
As many ounces as she did weigh
Of his own flesh pickt from his bones
Which made him sigh with bitter grones

His lady ask'd him why he grieved
He said my Jewel I received
The Sum of money of a Jew
With which I bought and purchased you

And now the time of payment's come
And since I cannot raise that sum
He'll have my flesh love weight for weight
Which makes my grief and sorrow great

Pish never mind him she Reply'd
We'll crofs the foaming ocean wide
Come on my love you've won my heart
My dear no one shall make us part

Then having croft the raging seas
They came on until by degrees
Unto German court they came
This English knight and royal dame

Unto the Emperor he told
The Story of the sum of gold
Which he had borrow'd of a Jew
And that for fear of Death he flew

The Emperor did then Direct
A Court for them and Shew'd respect
To his new guefs because they came
From England that best land of fame

Whilst there they lived in much delight
A Dutch Lord told the English knight
That he a Ton of Gold would lay
That he'd Enjoy his Lady gay

From her the Dutch Lord was to bring
A Rich and Costly Diamond ring
Which was to prove and testify
That he did with his lady lie

He try'd her favor to Obtain
But she with Scorn & high disdain
She did abhor his base intent
So to her Servant made he went

And told her that if she would Steal
Her Lady's ring and so conceal
The Same and bring it to him strait
She should Enjoy a fair estate

In hopes of such a large reward
The ring she stole then the dutch lord
Did carry it to the English knight
Who almost swooned at the sight

Then he run to his palace strait
And As he met Her at the gate
He flung her hedlong down the mote
& left her there to sink or float

As down the Stream She floating past
A miller took her up at last

Saving her life and Jewells too
Which was more than her husband new

Soon after this Enclos'd in Green
She like a warlike knight was seen
Well mounted on a warlike Stead
Unto the Court She Rode with Speed

And when the Emperor Beheld
What great Deportment she was fill'd
With admiration at the sight
She called herself an English Knight

The Emperor did then reply
Here is an english knight to see
for drowning of his lady gay
Quoth She I'll See him if I may

Twas granted & to him She came
& as She call'd him by the name
She said kind Sir be of good Cheer
Thy friend I'll be thou need not fear

Back to the Emperor She rides
& Says pray let this cause be tri'd
Once more for I'm In hopes to save
This english galeant from the grave

Twas granted and court being set
The dutch Lord came who seemed to swet
about the ring for he did fear
The truth would make his shame appear

And so it did for strait they call'd
The maid who on her knees did fall
Before the Court and there confefsed
The dutch Lords base unworthynefs

He hired me to steel the ring
Which he did to my mafter bring
And Said he had it of his wife
Which was the cause of all the Strife

The Court reply'd & it is so
The lady too for ought we know
May be alive therefore well Stay
His Sentence too another day

And you Dutch Lord pay him the ton
of Gold which he has fairly won
And So he did with Shame and grief
And then the knight obtained relief

The Dutch Lord to Revenge the Spright
Upon the noble English knight
Did send a letter out of hand
That to the Jew might understand

That he was at the German Court
Wherefore upon the base Report
The Jew then crofsd the Ocean wide
Refolved to be satisfy'd

As soon as Ere he first his Eyes
Upon the Knight with wrath he cries
Your hand and Seal I pray behold
Your flesh Ile have inftead of gold

With that Reply'd the knight in green
Pray let your articles be seen
Yes that they may Reply'd the Jew
For I'm Refolved to have my due

The knight in green said Mr. Jew
There's nothing here but flesh is your due

And see no drop of Blood you shed
For if you do off goes your head

The knight in Green got loud applause
In that he made him quit the cause
But telling him what Should Ensue
if that one drop of Blood he drew

With that reply'd the Emperor
Pray let me see it worthy Sir
Who did this Bloody Bond contrive
What cut him into takes alive

No sooner were these troubles past
But his wifes father came at last
Resolving he would have his life
For drowning his beloved wife

They Brought him from the prison then
Guarded by many armed men
Unto the place where he must die
The knight in green came riding by

And from his side his sword he drew
And run his gelding through & thro
Her father said why do you so
I say he is my own you know

I bought this golden tis well known
To all mankind he is my own
Therefore I may it is well known
Do what I please with whats my own

Here is A man arragned and cast
And brought to suffer death at last
Because my Daughter dear he slew
Perhaps he might what is that to you

You took your money when you sold
Your daughter for her weight in gold
Therefore he might it is well known
Do what he pleased with whats his own

And when her noble Father dear
This Royal arguments did here
Forgave him then Immediatly
Determin'd that he should not die

Then having changed her garments green
She deckt herself like a fair queen
Her Father and her Husband stait
Both knew her and their joys were great

Soon they did cary this report
Through all the Famous German Court
Had the Renowned English Knight
Had found his Charming beauty bright

The Emperor & Lord of Fame
With Cheerful hearts they did proclaim
A Universal Joy to See
He is Lady's life & Liberty

ɔpied literatim et punctatim from the Grandey Blankbook. This eighteenth century
ɑnuscript contains 132 pages of folksongs current during the American Revolution. It
ɑs the property successively of Edmund and Joseph Grandey of Panton, Vermont.

H. H. F., Collector
February 13, 1939

THE WIFE OF AUCHTERMUCHTY

There was a wealthy farmer
As I have heard them Say
As he went out a plowing
Twas on one Stormy day

The wind & Weather
Blew so cold He could no longer Stay
Then he went home unto his wife
And thus to her did Say

"As for you & and your Children
You live at home at ease
You do not do any work
But do just as you please
O you shall take your turn
About—or else I'll break
Your bones—Go early in the morning

So early the next morning
To plow with John she went
She left her Old man warm in bed—
The Children for to tend
He went into the kitchin
To fetch the Child a clout
The old Sow & pigs they did come in
A Shut (?) the house about

These pigs they wantd Serving
As you have often seen
They went into the dairy house
And Served themselves with Cream
The cream pots & the milk pans
They rattled all about—
The old Sow did the Churn fling down
Before he got them out

Then he took up the Churndasher
for to drive out the pigs
Some he hit Some he mist
and some he Broke their legs
He drove them out a swearing
Saying death Shall be your Doom—

The old Sow turned her head one Side and
Bit him on the Thumb

Then he went into the Parlour
For to do up his thumb
His Children they were squalling
And crying out for mamy
Your mam is gone to plow
& I am almost dead
One fell onto the floor & to them Before (?) the Bed

Then he went in & took his Child
And put it into bed
Then he went up & got his wheel
For to Begin his trade
He went out to wash a Clout
And hang the Same to dry
The tow took fire & burnt his wheel
His work went all awry

Then he got tired of womens work
On him that went so crofs
He'd go and call his wife in
He'd be no longer nufs
Then he went out like one stark mad—
To call his wife from plow
Young John he was a kifsin her
Behind the Barley mow

From the Grandey Blankbook loaned to H. H. F., February 13, 1939. Copied literatim
et punctatim, the British text:

YOU GENTLEMEN OF ENGLAND FARE

You gentlemen of England fare
Who stay at home free from all care
Oh little do you think or know

The dangers Seamen Undergo
They mile they Toil all on the way
They work like Turkish galley slaves

Twas on November the fourteenth day
When first our Admiral bore away
Intending for our native shore
The wind at west Southwest did roar
Attended by a dismal Sky
The seas they ran full mountains high

The Very first Land our Ships crew mde
It proved to be the old rams head
Which made us for to rejoice and bound
To see our flag staff in plymouth sound
But streching oer the fisher noes
Thinking to bring our palamoers

The tide of Ebb being quite run down
The current Strong to the west did run
Which made us for to Stomp and Swear
Our Goodly Ship She would not wear
The wind & the weather Encreasing sore
Which drive nine sail of our line on Shore

The firft was the Duke of north Cumberland
The Lion and the antelope
The eagle and the weasle too
Which caused Elizabeth for to rue
She ran stemlong the Lion broke
And sunk the orange at one Stroke

Now is to Come the worst of all
Our largest ship hand the greatest fall
The great croronation and all her men
Were lost and drowned except nineteen
Which was the mate with Eighteen more
Who in the longboat got on shore

The worst of loosing of lifes
is to our sweethearts and our wifes
Next to the nation it mus be
To loose nine Sail Such Ships as we
But Oh! the girl I love
I Hope She'll keep and constant prove

When I was young and crost in love
Which first caused me the Seas to rove
My parents they have crewel been
Would not let me Enjoy my queen
But oh! ye powers above
Help me to the girls I dearly love

Received by mail from James Copeland of Bridgeport, Connecticut.

H. H. F., Collector
July, 1949

The American Text

YE PARLIAMENT OF ENGLAND

You first consigned our commerce
And say our ships can't trade.
You then confined our seamen
And used them as your slaves.

Then you insulted Rogers
While cruising on the main
And hadn't we declared war
You'd tried it o'er again.

You thought our vessels were small
And Yankees couldn't fight
Until brave Hull your Guerrier took
And vanished from your sight.

The Wasp then took the Frolick.
You nothing said to that.

The Poiteiers being on the line,
Of course, she took her back.

Sung by Mr. Oscar Degreenia of West Cornwall, Connecticut, to Mrs. A. C. Beal an
H. H. F., Collecto
May 16, 1949

YOUNG BUT DAILY GROWING

"O father, dearest father, you've done to me much wrong;
You've married me to a man lots too young
For I'm twice twelve and he's scarcely thirteen.
He is young but he's daily a-growing,
He is young but he's daily a-growing."

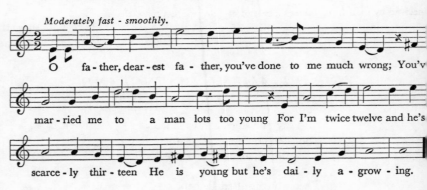

"O daughter, dearest daughter, I've done to you no wrong.
I've married you to a rich lord's son;
A rich lord's son. A wife you'd oughta be
Though he's young he's daily a-growing.
He is young but he's daily a-growing."

"O father, dearest father, if you think best,
We'll send him to school a year or two years.
I'll tie a blue ribbon around about his hat
So's to let the girls know that he is married,
So's to let the girls know that he is married."

She made him a shirt of the linen so fine.
She whipped it all over with her own hands,
And every stitch that she did put on,
"O my beany boy's a long time a-growing;
O my beany boy's a long time a-growing."

As she was a-passing her father's castle wall
She saw the school boys a-tossing up their ball;
She saw that her beany was the flower of them all
Though he's young but he's daily a-growing.
He was young but he was daily a-growing.

At the age of fourteen he was a married man,
At the age of fifteen his oldest son was born,
At the age of sixteen his grave was growing green
And that put an end to his growing.

As sung by Mr. Oscar Degreenia. Learned some sixty years before when a child in Barton,
Vermont. His father and mother both sang it but whether it came from Canada where
his father was born or from Glover, Vermont, where his mother was a native, he did
not know. Sung to Mrs. A. C. Beal and

H. H. F., Collector
May 16, 1949

MARY ALLING

(Child 84)

'Twas early in the springtime of the year
When all the flowers were blooming
A young man on his dying bed
In love with Mary Alling.

Slowly she rose, slowly she rose
And slowly she went to him.
When she got there, "Young man!" she said,
"I really think you're dying."

"A dying man I am not yet.
One kiss from you would save me."
"One kiss from me, you never shall have
If your heart was really a-breaking.

Verse. I. Narrative manner.

Twas ear-ly in the spring-time of the year when all the flow-ers were bloom-ing a young man on his dy-ing bed In love with Ma-ry All-ing.

Verse II.

Slow-ly she rose slow-ly she rose and slow-ly she went to him When she got there "Young man!" she said, "I real-ly think you're dy-ing."

"Do you remember in the dancing hall
When all the music were ringing
You danced around with all the rest
And slighted Mary Alling?

"Do you remember to your father's house
To a place called dwelling
You drank your wine with all the rest
And slighted Mary Alling?"
"You look to the head of my bed
There is a napkin hanging

Into it is my gold watch and chain—
It's all for Mary Alling.
"You look to the side of my bed.

There is a basin standing.
It quite overflows with my heart's blood
I shed for Mary Alling."

As she was standing in her father's gate
She heard the church bell tolling
And every time the church bell tolled
It sounded "Mary Alling."

As she was standing in her father's gate
She saw the hearse a-coming.
"Pull down, pull down, that cold, cold corpse,
So I can gaze upon him."

And the more she gazed and the more she scorned
And the more she gazed upon him
Until the girls did all cry out,
A shame on Mary Alling.

Unto her mother she did go
And unto her did say,
"O mother, mother, make my bed
Go and make it long and narrow,
My true love died for me to-day
I'll die for him to-morrow."

Unto her father she did go
And unto him did say,
"O father, father, dig my grave
Go and dig it long and narrow.
My true love died for me to-day,
I'll die for him to-morrow."

And on his grave there grew a rose
And onto hers a briar.

They grew so tall, they grew so tall
And twined away together.

As sung by Mr. Oscar Degreenia of West Cornwall, Connecticut, to Mrs. A. C. Beal and
H. H. F., Collector
May 16, 1949

LORD RANDALL

(Child 12)

"Where have you been, Young Nelson, my son?
Where have you been, my own pretty one?"
"I have been to see my sweetheart.
Mother, make my bed soon
For I'm poisoned to the heart
And am bound to lie down."

"What did you have for your dinner, Young Nelson, my son?" etc.
"A piece of rattlesnake." etc.

"What do you will to your brother, young Nelson, my son?" etc.
"A black mourning suit." etc.

"What do you will to your sister, young Nelson, my son?" etc.
"A black silk dress." etc.

"What do you will to your sweetheart, young Nelson, my son?" etc.
"A rope to hang her." etc.

"What do you will to your father, young Nelson, my son?" etc.
"Horse and cart." etc.

"What do you will to your mother, young Nelson, my son?" etc.
"The rest of my things." etc.

"Where do you want your bed made, young Nelson, my son?" etc.
"Under the green cherry tree." etc.

"What do you want to be covered up with, young Nelson, my son?" etc.
"Red sand and dirt." etc.

Sung by Mr. Oscar Degreenia of West Cornwall, Connecticut, to H. H. F. and Mrs.
A. C. Beal, as sung by his parents to their eight children, living in a log cabin in Barton,
Vermont. Mr. Degreenia has lived the last 17 years in West Cornwall.

H. H. F., Collector
May 16, 1949

ANDREW BATAN

(Child 250)

There were three brothers in merry Scotland;
Three brothers they were all three
And they cast lots from one to the other
To see which the robber would be.

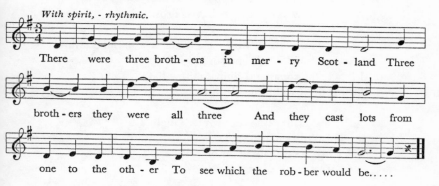

The lot did fall on Andrew Batan,
The youngest of the three,
That he would go robbing all on the high sea
To maintain his two brothers and he.

As he was sailing one cold winter's night
A light did soon appear.
They saw a ship sailing far off and far off
And at length it came sailing near.

"Who art, who art," cried Capting Charles Stewart,
"Who art that's sailing so nigh?"
"We are the bold robbers from fair Scotland.
Will you please for to let us pass by?"

"O no, O no, that thing we never shall do,
That thing we never shall do.
Your ship and your cargo we'll all take away
And salt water your bodies shall see.
Your ship and your cargo we'll all take away
And salt water your bodies shall see."

The news soon came on England's home shore
(King George he wore the crown.)
That the rich merchant's goods had been taken away
And the crew and the captain was drowned,
That the rich merchant's goods had been taken away
And the crew and the captain was drowned.

"Go and build me a ship," cries Captain Charles Stewart,
"Go and build it safe and sure.
I'll take the command from Andrew Batan
Or my life I will never endure."

As he was sailing one cold winter's night
A light did soon appear.
They saw a ship sailing far off and far off
And at length it came sailing near.

"Who art, who art?" cries Captain Charles Stewart,
"Who are, that's sailing so nigh?"
"We are the bold robbers from fair Scotland.
Will you please for to let us pass by?"

"O no, O no, that thing we never shall do;
That thing we never shall do.
Your ship and your cargo we'll all take away
And your bodies fair England will see."

"Come on, come on," cried Andrew Batan,
"We fear you not one pin
For we're brass without that makes the fine show
But we are all steel within."

Broadsides, broadsides they quickly put on
And cannons loud did roar
And Capting Charles Stewart took Andrew Batan
And they hung him on England's own shore.

. But she knew what she was doing. Soon he began, in that tune, to sing
n Castyle There Lived a Lady" and it was the old tale of the lady's fan in
 lion's den. In New England we have several forms of the song but not in
at tune. In quoting the words, I end each stanza when the tune comes its
mplete circle.

That same day, I drove on to Naugatuck to hear songs known to Mrs.
lwin C. White. She had sent me words to "The Two Sisters" and I wanted
 hear them in her tune. In New England we have yet to find a form of the
dest way it may have been known, an eerie version wherein the eldest
ughter of a king drowns her youngest sister, hoping to win the love of her
itor. She buries the princess under a thorn tree. Along comes a shepherd boy
d from a branch of the tree he makes a pipe on which to play tunes he
ows. But, however he fingers the stops, he can never play what he intends.
stead the instrument sings of the tragic death of the young maiden. The
untry people are amazed. The wonder eventually comes to the attention of
e king. The shepherd boy is brought before him to play his willful pipe. Just
tribution follows, to the satisfaction of all ballad singers.

This song is known in the Faroe Islands, in Sweden, Denmark, and Nor-
ay, as well as throughout the British Isles. Some years ago, a bedridden Irish-
oman was singing it to me the way she learned it in her childhood in County
ork. In the nearby kitchen a Polish neighbor was "reddying-up" for her,
ith one ear to all the old tales. Suddenly she stood in the doorway. "My
other knows that song in Polish," she volunteered and verse by verse, she
anslated what was to be, among scholars, the first-known Polish form of that
ncient ballad.*

---

* Bulletin No. 10, 1935, of Folksong Society of the Northeast.

In Naugatuck, Mrs. White also sang the tender song of "Christ in
Garden" where, years ago, ballad singers put themselves in Christ's place a
sang about Gethsemane. The tune strongly carries the pathos.

We have only a few folk versions of Christian legends. In Cheshire, "T
Seven Joys of Mary" is known to Mrs. C. G. Erskine, formerly of Dixfie
Maine.

As sung by Mr. Ralph Lewis, Agamenticus Section, York, Maine. Learned from
grandfather. Incomplete.

M. Olney, Collec
September 22, 19

CAPTAIN WARD AND THE RAINBOW
(Child 287)

Come all you jolly sailors bold,
Who lives by tuck of drum;
I'll tell you of a rank robber
That on the seas has come.
His name it is called Captain Ward
Like well it doth appear
There has not been a rank robber
Found out ten thousand year.

He wrote a letter to a king,
On the first of January,
To see if he could accept of him
And all his jolly company.
And for a ransom he would pay
Ten thousand pounds in gold
"Oh no, oh no," then said the king,
"For no such thing can be
For you have been a rank robber
A rover on the sea.

"For you deceived the king of France
And then the King of Spain.
For how can you prove true to us
When you proved false to them?"
Then says Captain Ward, "My boys,
We put to sea again
To see what prizes we can find
On the coast of France and Spain."

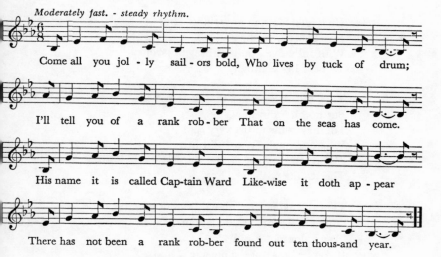

Moderately fast. - steady rhythm.

Come all you jol - ly sail - ors bold, Who lives by tuck of drum;

I'll tell you of a rank rob - ber That on the seas has come.

His name it is called Cap-tain Ward Like-wise it doth ap - pear

There has not been a rank rob-ber found out ten thous-and year.

They sailed East, they sailed West
(can't think)
They espied a lofty ship
A-sailing from the West
Loaded with silks and satins
And cambrics of the best.
Then they bore down on her,
A-thinking of no such thing.
They robbed them of their merchandise
And bid them tell the King.

And when the King did hear of this
His heart was grief full sore

To think his ships would not get pass
And as they had done before.

The King caused the old
....
And a worthy ship of fame
The Rainbow she was called
And the Rainbow was her home.

He rigged her and he freighted her
And sent her to the sea,
With fully five hundred brave mariners
To bear her company.

They sailed East and they sailed West
But nothing did they spy
Till they came to the very spot
Where Captain Ward did lie.
"Who is the owner of that ship?"
The Rainbow then did cry.

That the gallant Rainbow shot out on either side
"Fire on, fire on," said Captain Ward,
"We value not a pin
If you be brass on the outside
We are good steel within!"

We shot and shot in the morning
Shot and shot in vain. . . .

ung by Mr. Oscar Degreenia of West Cornwall, Connecticut, to Mrs. A. C. Beal and

H. H. F., Collector
May 16, 1949

IN CASTYLE THERE LIVED A LADY

In Castyle there lived a lady,
Lady of a high degree,
Saying, "Never a man, a man of honor
Never a man shall marry me."

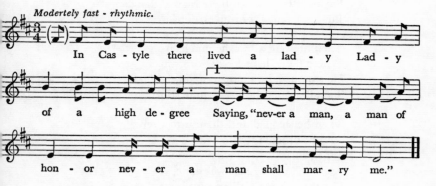

Till she saw two loving brothers
Came this fair damsel for to see.
Then up speaks this bold sea lady
"How can I be but one man's bride?

"Now ye brothers, come to-morrow
And the question I'll decide."
Parted those two loving brothers
Thinking of their silly doom,

While she lie musing on her pillow
Until mornin' light did come.
Then she called for coach and horses.
For the lion's den was she.

She threw her fan all in the dungeon
Where fierce lions looked so grim
Saying, "Which one will get it will be my bride."

Then up speaks this bold sea captain,
"Madam, your wishes I can't improve
For in that den there is great danger
And my life I'll not lose for love."

Then up speaks this bold lieutenant,
Bold lieutenant from the war,
Saying, "In that den there is great danger
But your fan, I'll bring or die."

Then he went all in the dungeon
Where fierce lions looked so grim.
He stomped, he stomped upon the floor
Till all around him was quite still.

Then he stooped and the fan recovered
And he brought it safe agin.
When she saw her love a-coming
And no harm to him was done,
She threw herself all on his bosom
Saying, "Here's the gift that you have won."

Then up speaks this bold sea captain
Like a man that's troubled in mind
Saying, "Off in some far lands I'll wander
Where no man my body'll find."

A fragment was recorded as sung by Mrs. Edwin C. White of Naugatuck, Connecticut. Within a day, Mrs. White mailed the rest of the song, having remembered all of it as sung in her childhood by her mother.

H. H. F., Collector
May 17, 1949

THE TWO SISTERS
(Child 10)

There was a miller lived in the west, bow down, bow down;
There was a miller lived in the west, declaring unto me,
There was a miller lived in the west;
He had two daughters, some of the best.
I will be true, true to my love
If my love will be true to me.

(Follow pattern throughout verses)

The miller he courted the eldest first, etc.
But still he loved the youngest best. etc.

To the youngest he gave the gay gold ring, etc.
And to the eldest he gave nothing. etc.

To the youngest he gave the ruffled cap, etc.
And the eldest she got mad at that. etc.

The eldest said, "I'll be his bride." etc.
The youngest she sat down and cried. etc.

They wandered down to the river's brim, etc.
The eldest pushed the youngest in. etc.

She floated down to the miller's dam, etc.
The miller he saw the same. etc.

The miller he threw out his line and hook, etc.
And drawed her from the watery brook. etc.

Hand in hand to the church they went, etc.
They took their vows and were content. etc.

The eldest rushed to the river side, etc.
She dove, she sank and thus she died. etc.

As sung by Mrs. Edwin C. White of Naugatuck, Connecticut.

H. H. F., Collect
May 17, 1949

CHRIST IN THE GARDEN

All nature was sinking in silence to rest.
The sun in its glory sank low in the west.
I walked in the garden and there on the ground
Was the loneliest creature that ever was found.

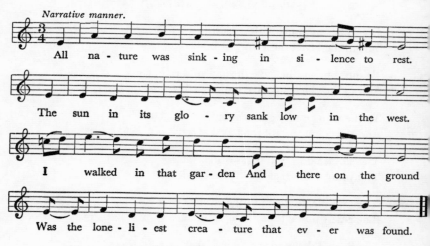

Narrative manner.

All na - ture was sink - ing in si - lence to rest.

The sun in its glo - ry sank low in the west.

I walked in that gar - den And there on the ground

Was the lone - li - est crea - ture that ev - er was found.

His mantle was wet with the dews of the night;
His locks by pale moonlight shone glittering and bright;
His eyes, full of anguish to heaven were raised
While angels descending in pity did gaze.

His form it was bowed but not with the years,
While down o'er his bosom rolled sweat, blood and tears.

I gazed upon him and I asked him his name.
He answered, " 'Tis Jesus; from Heaven I came.

"I am thy Redeemer, for thee I must die.
The cup is most bitter but can not pass by.
Thy sins which are many are all laid on me
And all this deep anguish I suffer for thee."

I knelt down before Him and to Him I did cry,
"Lord, save a poor sinner! Save, Lord, or I die."
He looked upon me and said to me, "Live.
Thy sins which are many I freely forgive."

I sped from the garden to spread it abroad.
I shouted salvation and glory to God.
I am now on my journey to mansions above.
My heart's full of pity, of joy, peace and love.

I soon shall see Jesus in loved Paradise.
I'll gaze on that creature with unclouded eyes.

ung by Mrs. C. G. Erskine of Cheshire, Connecticut, as her grandmother, Orinda Town-
end, born in 1828, used to sing it in Dixfield, Maine.

H. H. F., Collector
October 1, 1939

THE SEVEN JOYS OF MARY

The first joy that Mary had
It was the joy of one:
To see her Son, Jesus, her own loving Son,
Her own loving Son. What a joy that must be,
Father, Son and Holy One
And Christ eternally.

The second joy that Mary had,
It was the joy of two,
To see her Son, Jesus, her own loving Son

Disputing with a Jew. What a joy that must be,
Father, Son and Holy One
And Christ eternally.

The first joy that Ma-ry had, It was the joy of
one. To see her Son, Je-sus, her own lov-ing Son,
Her own lov-ing Son. What a joy that must be Fath-er
Son and Ho-ly One and Christ E-ter-nal-ly.

The third joy that Mary had,
It was the joy of three,
To see her Son, Jesus, her own loving Son
Nail-ed to the tree. What a joy that must be,
Father, Son and Holy One
And Christ eternally.

The fourth joy that Mary had,
It was the joy of four,
To see her Son, Jesus, her own loving Son,
Preaching to the poor. What a joy that must be,
Father, Son and Holy One
And Christ eternally.

The fifth joy that Mary had,
It was the joy of five,
To see her Son, Jesus, her own loving Son,
Make the dead alive. What a joy that must be,
Father, Son and Holy One
And Christ eternally.

The sixth joy that Mary had,
It was the joy of six,
To see her Son, Jesus, her own loving Son
Bear the crucifix. What a joy that must be,
Father, Son and Holy One
And Christ eternally.

The seventh joy that Mary had,
It was the joy of seven,
To see her Son, Jesus, her own loving Son,
Ascending into heaven. What a joy that must be,
Father, Son and Holy One
And Christ eternally.

rs. C. G. Erskine of Cheshire, Connecticut, learned this cumulative song from her
andmother.

H. H. F., Collector
October 1, 1939

THE TWELVE DAYS OF CHRISTMAS

The first day of Christmas, my true love sent to me
One plump partridge on a pear tree

(*the song is cumulative ending with*)

The eleventh day of Christmas, my true love sent to me
Eleven maids a-sweeping,
Ten bulls a-bellowing,
Nine lords a-leaping,
Eight ladies dancing,
Seven swans a-swimming,
Six geese a-laying,
Five gold rings,
Four French horns,
Three turtle doves,
Two fine ducks,
One plump partridge on a pear tree.

The first day of Christ-mas my true love sent to me

One plump par-tridge on a pear tree The sec-ond day of Christmas

true love sent to me Two fine ducks One plump par-tridge on

pear tree The third day of Christ-mas my true-love sent to me

Three tur-tle doves Two fine ducks One plump par-tridge on a pear-tree

The fourth day of Christ-mas my true-love sent to me Four French ho

Three tur-tle doves Two fine ducks One plump par-tridge on a pear-tree

The fifth day of Christ-mas my true-love sent to me.

Five gold rings Four French horns Three tur-tle doves Two fine ducks

One plump par-tridge on a pear tree The sixth day of Christ-mas my

true-love sent to me   Six geese a-lay-ing   Five gold rings,

Four French hens, Three tur-tle doves Two fine ducks   One plump

par-tridge on a   pear-tree   The Sev-enth day of Christ-mas my

true love sent to me   Sev-en swans a-swim-ing Six geese a-lay-ing

Five gold rings Four French horns Three tur-tle doves Two fine ducks, One plump

par-tridge on a   pear-tree   The Eighth day of Christ-mas my

true-love sent to me   Eight la-dies danc-ing Sev-en swans a-swim-ing

Six geese a-lay-ing   Five gold rings Four French horns Three tur-tle doves

Two fine ducks   One plump par-tridge on a   pear tree

The Ninth day of Christ-mas my true-love sent to   me

Nine lords a-leap-ing Eight la-dies danc-ing Sev-en swans a-swim-ing

Six geese a-lay-ing Five gold rings Four French horns Three tur-tle doves

Two fine ducks One plump par-tridge on a pear-tree

The Tenth day of Christ-mas my true-love sent to me

Ten bulls a-bel-low-ing Nine lords a-leap-ing Eight lad-ies

danc-ing Sev-en swans a-swim-ing Six geese a-lay-ing.

Five gold rings Four French horns Three tur-tle doves

Two fine ducks, One plump par-tridge on a pear-tree.

. . . In Vermont, we have from a native of Northumberland, "St. Stephe
and Herod," known in his family for two centuries. Possibly we have anothe
Christian legend in "The Bold Fisherman" as known to Mr. Charles Finne
more of Bridgewater, Maine. It has all the elements which led Miss Luc
Broadwood, of the English Folk-Song Society to consider them possibly "
vulgar and secularized transmutation of a mediaeval allegorical origina
Familiar elements of the Gnostic and Early Christian Mystical literature ar
The River, Sea, Royal Fisher, Three Vestures of Light (Robes of Glory), th

:ognition and Adoration by the illuminated humble soul and the Free
don. Also the early Fathers of the Christian Church wrote of the baptized
nbers as 'fish' emerged from the waters of baptism."*

There is rhythm of the sea in the tune. . . .

s ballad was recorded in Burlington, Vermont, as remembered by Mr. George L.
vards from the singing of his grandmother of Seaton, East Riding, Yorkshire, England.

H. H. F., Collector
October 16, 1934

ST. STEPHEN AND HEROD

(Child 22)

St. Stephen was a serving-man
In Herod's royal hall.
He serv-ed him with meat and wine
That doth to kings befall.

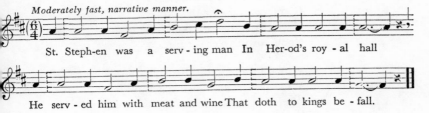

Moderately fast, narrative manner.

St. Steph-en was a serv-ing man In Her-od's roy-al hall

He serv-ed him with meat and wine That doth to kings be-fall.

He was serving him with meat, one day,
With a boar's head in his hand,
When he saw a star come from the East
And over Bethlehem stand.

St. Stephen was a righteous man
And in his faith was bold.
He was waiting for the birth of Christ
As by the prophets told.

* *Journal* of the English Folk-Song Society, Vol. V, p. 132.

He cast the Boar's head on the floor
And let the server fall;
He said, "Behold a child is born
That is better than we all."

Then quickly he went to Herod's room
And unto him did say,
"I am leaving thee, King Herod,
And will proclaim thy wicked ways."

As sung by Mr. Charles Fennimore of Bridgewater, Maine.

M. Olney, Collec
May 7, 1942

THE BOLD FISHERMAN

As I walked out one May morning
Down by the riverside;
'Twas there I saw a bold fisherman
Come rowing o'er the tide.
Come rowing o'er the tide,
'Twas there I saw a bold fisherman
Come rowing o'er the tide.

"Good morning, brother fisherman,
What brings you down this way?"
"I come to court some lady gay
From o'er the rolling sea." Etc.

He tied his boat unto the strand
And straightway to her went,
He took her by the lily-white hand,
Which was his full intent. Etc.

Then he pulled off his morning gown
And throwed it on the ground;
When then she saw three chains of gold
Around his neck hung down. Etc.

She fell a-pon her bended knee,
"O pardon, sir, I crave,
For calling you a bold fisherman
From o'er the rowing wave." Etc.

With grace and rhythm.

As I walked out one May morn - ing Down by the
riv - er side; Twas there I saw a bold fish - er-man Come
row - ing o'er the tide. Come row - ing o'er the tide Twas
there I saw a bold fish - er - man Come row-ing o'er the tide.

"Now nothing have you done amiss
That has offended me;
But come unto your father's house
And married we will be." Etc.

. . One singer passes me on to another. Mrs. White spoke of her brother in
Warren, who might, better than she, remember their mother's songs. So
another day found me with Mr. Edward Richards, who took time off from
the very pleasant home he was building with his own hands, to remember
and sing an unusual form of "Wife Wrapped in Wether's Skin," "Barney's
Courtship" and the early American "Sword of Bunker Hill." About that
"Sword of Bunker Hill" he said that when his mother came to

"A captain raised his blade at me.
I tore it from his hand"

goose pimples would start from his toes and go all over him, when he wa
youngster. Some years later, after he had married and had a family, wl
again he heard his mother sing that song, goose pimples rose again in t
fight for freedom. It is a tremendously stirring event, when he sings it.

In New London I came upon old sea-going chanteys known to Capt
Christopher Culver. He sang the hauling songs, "Santa Anna," "Shenandoa
"Blow the Man Down," "Whiskey Johnnie," "Sally Brown" and the fine
"Homeward Bound Chantey." But one "Old Horse, Old Horse" is less cc
monly printed and known. Captain Culver prefaced his singing with, "T
commemorates a trip, on the old 'Julius Caesar,' Rattler Morgan (he v
Cap'n) out of Groton coming into New London after a three years' cruis
and they got pretty nearly out of grub; 'n the cook went to the harness-c
with his chain hook and pushed it around in there, and finally he hooked ii
something, hauled it up and it was a horse's head. So he took it and pu
into his coppers and cooked it and sent it along to the fo'castle, and
fo'castle wag was there. He looked down and said 'Old Hoss, old Hoss, h
came you here?' and the horse replies in this song."

This song is in the hymn tune of "All Hail the Power of Jesus' Nam
A longer description of this same song is in a footnote in Richard Her
Dana's *Two Years Before The Mast.* . . .

This song must have suffered a sea-change by the time it was heard
Mrs. Henry Clark of Suffield, Connecticut. Then it was called "The S
Horse Song." She writes: "It was given me years ago by Cliff Mosher,
sea-going cook who I think came from Maine, although he shipped in a bc
on which I sailed to San Francisco, from New London." The tune resemb
"Maryland, My Maryland."

urnished by Mr. Edward Richards of Warren, Connecticut, as he remembered the sing-
1g of his mother, a native of those parts.

H. H. F., Collector
August 31, 1949

WIFE WRAPPED IN WETHER'S SKIN

(Child 277)

There was an old man lived in the West
    Dan-do, Dan-do,
There was an old man lived in the West
Who had a wife she was none of the best
    Dan-do.
Nickety rumpter klinety klunk—
Ter kling-go

(Follow pattern for next verses)

One morning the old man came in from plow, etc.
Saying, "Wife, is breakfast ready now?" etc.

"There's a crust of bread lies on the shelf, etc.
If you want anything, go help yourself." etc.

The old man went out to his sheepfold, etc.
He drawed an old wether up to the pole. etc.

He drawed an old wether up to the pin, etc.
And quickly he took off its skin. etc.

He put the skin around his wife's back, etc.
He took his whip and he made it crack. etc.

"I'll tell my mother and then I'll see
How cruel you are whipping me." etc.

"You can tell your mother and all your kin
That I'm only a-tanning this old sheep skin." etc.

As sung by Mr. Edward Richards of Warren, Connecticut.

H. H. F., Collec
August 31, 1949

BARNEY AND KATEY

'Twas a cold winter's night and the wind it was brawling.
The snow like a sheet covered cabin and sty
When Barney flew over the hills to his darlin'
And he tapped at the window where Katey did lie.

"Arrrrrrray, jewel," says he, "are ye sleepin' or wakin'?
'Tis a bitter cold night and me coat it is thin.
The storm is a-brewin' and the frost is a-bakin'.
O, sweet Katey, darlin', won't ye please let me in?"

"O, Barney," says Katey, she spake through the winda.
"Why do ye come talkin' me out of me bed?

To be sure it is a shame and a sin to ye.
'Tis whiskey, not love that's got into yer head.

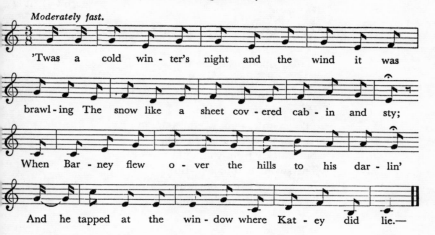

Moderately fast.

'Twas a cold win-ter's night and the wind it was brawl-ing The snow like a sheet cov-ered cab-in and sty; When Bar-ney flew o-ver the hills to his dar-lin' And he tapped at the win-dow where Kat-ey did lie.—

"O think of the time of me name ye'd be tender.
Consider it's night and there's nobody in.
What has a poor girl but her name to defend her?
Ray no, Barney Avouren, I won't let ye in."

"O cushla," says he, "in me eye there's a fountain
To weep for the wrong I would lay at yer door.
Yer heart is as pure as the shnaw on the mountain
And Barney would die to preserve it as pure.

"I'll go to me home though the winter winds face me.
I'll whistle them off for I'm happy within
And the words of my Katey shall comfort and bless me,
'Ray no, Barney Aver, I won't let ye in.' "

As sung by Mr. Edward Richards of Warren, Connecticut.

H. H. F., Collecte
August 31, 1949

THE SWORD OF BUNKER HILL

He lay upon his dying bed.
His eyes were waxing dim
When with a feeble voice he called
His weeping son to him.
"Weep not, my boy," the veteran cried,
"I bow to Heav'n's high will,
But quickly from yon antlers bring
The sword of Bunker Hill;
But quickly from yon antlers bring
The sword of Bunker Hill."

Sharp phrasing, declamatory manner.

He lay up-on his dy - ing bed. His eyes were wax - ing dim

When with a fee - ble voice he called His weep-ing son to him.

"Weep not, my boy!" the vet-'ran cried "I bow to Heav'ns high will

But quick-ly from yon ant - lers bring The sword of Bunk - er Hill

But quick-ly from yon ant - lers bring The sword of Bunk - er Hill."

The sword was brought, the soldier's eyes
Lit with a sudden flame
And as he grasped that ancient blade
He murmured Warren's name.
Then said, "My boy, I leave you gold
But what is richer still
I leave you. . . . mark me, mark me, boy,
The sword of Bunker Hill;
I leave you. . . . mark me, mark me, boy,
The sword of Bunker Hill.

"Twas on that dread immortal day
We dared the Briton band.
A captain raised his blade at me.
I tore it from his hand,
And as the glorious battle raged
It lightened freedom's will
For, boy, the God of freedom blessed
The sword of Bunker Hill;
For, boy, the God of freedom blessed
The sword of Bunker Hill.

"O, keep the sword," his accents broke.
A smile, and he was dead
But still he held that cherished blade
Upon his dying bed.
The son remains, the sword remains
And in its glory still
There's many millions bless the sire
And sword of Bunker Hill;
There's many millions bless the sire
And sword of Bunker Hill.

As known to Mrs. Henry M. Clark, King's Field, Suffield, Connecticut.

H. H. F., Collec
March, 1950

THE SALT HORSE SONG

"Oh horse, oh horse, what brought you here?
You carted stone for many a year
With kicks and cuffs and ill abuse
Now salted down for sailors' use."

There you find him in damn great junks (or "chunks")
Between the mainmast and the pumps.
You pick him up with great surprise
And throw him down and damn his eyes;

And gnaw the meat from off the bones
And throw the rest to Davey Jones.
Now if you don't believe this story's true
Look in the barr'l and you'll find his shoe.

Sung by Captain Christopher Culver of New London, Connecticut, at the age of 81.

H. H. F., Collectc
May, 1949

OLD HOSS, OLD HOSS

"Old hoss, old hoss, how came you here?
    And they say so; they say so;
Old hoss, old hoss, how came you here?
    That good old man."

"From Sackerap to Portland Pier,
    And they say so; they say so;
I carted stun this many a year.
    That good old man.

"At length grown old from sore abuse,
    And they say so; they say so;

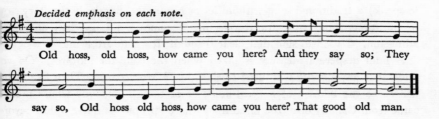

Decided emphasis on each note.

Old hoss, old hoss, how came you here? And they say so; They
say so, Old hoss old hoss, how came you here? That good old man.

> They salted me for sailors' use.
> That good old man.

> "Abaft, a-mainmast, stand a-pump,
>   And they say so; they say so;
> There stands that cask of old salt junk.
>   That good old man.

> "They pick me up and gnaw my bones,
>   And they say so; they say so;
> And throw me then to Davy Jones,
>   That good old man."

. . Folk ballads *are* migrants. They are like the frogs of which Miss Margaret Shipman of Lee, Massachusetts, writes: "Ed Shipman came from Connecticut to Massachusetts. A descendant, Mrs. Betsey Eaton Shipman, grandmother to Miss Shipman of Lee, tells of a time when frogs migrated overland throughout New England in such numbers that they frightened the farmers." She remembers only this one line of a song called "The Battle of the Frogs in New England" in speaking of one of the farmers:

> "A pound of good powder and bullets forgot."

Certainly there is nothing that reverts to Homer's description in his "Battle of the Frogs!" We have this much and no more.

Being migrants, ballads are unpredictable. One aspect, however, can be reckoned with. Folk ballads know no state boundaries. The collector may be in the front parlor of some remote farmhouse, her machine winding up (so to speak) a traditional song without let or hindrance. Suddenly the story stop in mid-tune. The pause for recollecting becomes a hiatus, then an aghas admission. "I used to sing that clear through. It's gone from me!"

A final desperate measure is taken when the collector inquires, "Do you remember anyone else who used to sing this?" More pauses. Then like as no will come the address of a great-aunt, or of Susie Somebody whose mother came from Canady or of the hired man whose "people" still live uphill beyond the mailboxes at the crossroads.

Miles away, there lies the faint prospect of hearing the rest of the unfinished ballad. As often as not, the singer is in another state. One instance among many was the case of Mrs. Lily Delorme (now deceased) whom Miss Olney visited at the kind invitation of Mrs. Marjorie Porter of Plattsburg, New York when Mrs. Delorme was living in Cadyville, New York. She sang eighteen Child ballads that were earlier known in her family when they lived in Starksboro, Vermont. Six of them seem natural to this book, so we included the Child ballads: "Earl Brand" (7), "Two Brothers" (49), "Unquiet Grave" (78), "Willie, of Winsbury" (100), "Braes of Yarrow" (214), "John o. Hazelgreen" (293).

Frequently a ballad is found far afield from the seeming origin of its events It seldom takes root in its native heath. . . .

As sung by Mrs. Lily Delorme of Cadyville, New York. Mrs. Delorme was born in Schuyler Falls, New York, in 1869. Her father was born in Starksboro, Vermont, her mother in Schuyler Falls. This ballad was learned in her home as a child.

M. Olney, Marjorie Porter, Collector
August 16, 1942

LORD WILLIAM AND LADY MARGARET
(Child 7)

"Lie down, lie down," Lord William cried
"And hold my steed in hand
For betwixt your father and your seven brothers bold
I quicklie make a stand."

"O stop, O stop, Lord William," she cried,
"I fear that you've been slain
And I fear my seven brothers are slain
And my father's been likewise slain."

Strict tempo.

"Lie down lie down, Lord Wil - liam cried," And
hold my steed in hand For be-'twixt your fath - er and your
sev - en broth - ers bold I quick - lie make them stand.

Then she taen out her handkerchief
That was of the holland so fine
And she did up her father's bloody wounds
That run as red as wine.

"Now make my bed, Lady mother," he said,
"And make it broad and neat
And lay Lady Margaret by my side
That sounder I may sleep."

Lord William died long in the night,
Lady Margaret long in the day
And they took them both home to St. Mary's church
And laid them in the clay.

Out of Lady Margaret's grave there grew a primrose
And out of the knight's a briar
And they linked and they tied in a true lover's knot
And withered away together.

Sung by Mrs. Lily Delorme of Cadyville, New York.

M. Olney, Marjorie Porter, Collector
August 16, 1943

MARTYR JOHN

(Child 49)

It was Martyr John who died of late
By his older brother's hand
As he walked o'er to take the air
And to view the pleasant land.

Narrative manner.

It was Mar - tyr John who died of late By his
old - er broth - er's hand As he walked o'er to
take the air And to view the pleas - ant land.

"O brother dear, when shall we return
From a-viewing the pleasant land?"
He answered him, "You never can return
For I have mercy none."

"Then what will you tell to my old father
When he'll call for his son John?"
"O I'll tell him that you've gone to the merry Greenwood
A-learning your hounds to run."

"Then what will you tell to my old mother
When she calls for her son John?"
"O I'll tell her that you've gone to fair Starksborotown
Your lessons for to learn."

"Then what will you to tell my pretty Susan
When she calls for her true-love John?"
"O I'll tell her that you are dead and in your grave laid
Never, never more to return."

Then he drew his dagger from his side
And he pierced his brother through
And he laid him down by the clear running brook
Saying: "Now, there's an end of you!"

Then he went home to his old father
Who said, "Where is my son John?"
"O he is in the merry Greenwood
A-learning his hounds to run."

And then upspoke his old mother
Saying: "Where is my son John?"
"O he has gone to fair Starksborotown
His lessons for to learn."

And then upspoke his pretty Susan
Saying, "Where is my true love John?"
"O he is dead and in his grave laid
Never, never more to return."

O she took her dagger in her hand
And she run along the clear running brook
And she run to the place where in the field
And the birds were in their nests.

And she mourned her true love out of his grave
O I'm sure that he could not rest.

"O what do you want, my pretty Susan,
O why do you mourn for me?"
"One kiss from your clay-cold lips
It's all that I want of thee."

"Go home! Go home! my pretty Susan
And worry no more for me
For you must have known from the day of your doom
I never can return to you."

Sung by Mrs. Lily Delorme of Cadyville, New York.

M. Olney, Marjorie Porter, Collect
August 16, 1943

COLD BLOWS THE WIND

(Child 78)

Cold blows the winter's wind, sweetheart,
Cold blows the drops of rain;
I never had but one sweetheart
And in the greenwood she was slain.

Cold blows the win-ter's wind sweet-heart, Cold blows the drops of rain; I
nev - er had but one Sweet-heart And in the green-wood she was slain.

I'll do as much for my sweetheart
As any young man may;
I'll sit all on her grave and mourn
A twelvemonth and a day.

A twelvemonth and a day being past,
Her ghost began to speak:
"Why sit upon my grave and mourn
And will not let me sleep?

"What do you want of me, sweetheart?
What do you want of me, I pray?"

"One kiss, one kiss of your clay cold lips
And that is all I want of thee."

"My lips are colder than clay, sweetheart,
My breath I'm sure is not strong.
If one kiss of my clay cold lips you have,
Your time, it won't be long."

As sung by Mrs. Lily M. Delorme of Cadyville, New York.

M. Olney, Marjorie Porter, Collectors
December 8, 1941

JOHNNY BARBOUR
(Child 100)

This lady was seated in her father's castle hall,
A-viewing the ships coming in;
"O daughter, dear!" her father said,
"Your cheeks look pale and thin,
Your cheeks look pale and thin.

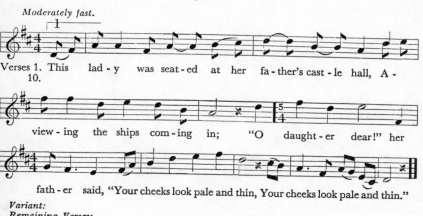

Moderately fast.

Verses 1. This lad-y was seat-ed at her fa-ther's cast-le hall, A-
10.
view-ing the ships com-ing in; "O daught-er dear!" her
fath-er said, "Your cheeks look pale and thin, Your cheeks look pale and thin."

Variant:
Remaining Verses:

"Is it any sickness you have got,
Or in love with a young man?"
"It is not sickness I have got,
But in love with a young man,
But in love with a young man."

"Is he a lord or is he a duke,
Or a man of honor and fame?'
"No, he's neither lord nor duke nor a man of honor and fame,
But he is one of your bold sea-boys,
John Barbour is his name."

"Then I'll call together my merry-men all,
By one, by two and by three,
And tomorrow morning at ten o'clock,
High hang-ed he shall be,
High hang-ed he shall be."

"O say not so, dear father," she said,
"O say not so unto me,
For if you hang John Barbour," she said,
"No good you'll get of me,
No good you'll get of me."

Then he calls together his merrymen all,
By one, by two and by three,
John Barbour being the very first man,
O the very last man was he,
O the very last man was he.

And when John Barbour he came out,
His suit was of the green,
With his coal black eyes a-rolling in his head
And his skin as fair as a queen,
And his skin as fair as a queen.

"I blame you not, dear daughter," he said,
"I blame you not," said he,
"For if I were one of the female sex,

His companion I would be,
His companion I would be."

"Will you marry my daughter, John Barbour," he said,
"And take her by the hand,
And walk and talk and sit with her,
Be an heir to my houses and lands,
Be an heir to my houses and lands?"

"Yes, I'll marry your daughter," John Barbour said,
"And take her by the hand,
I will walk and talk and sit with her,
But a fig for your houses and lands,
But a fig for your houses and lands.

"Although I'm called John Barbour here,
I'm the Duke of New Cumberland;
And before you can give her one guinea,
I can give her five hundred pounds,
I can give her five hundred pounds."

As sung by Mrs. Lily Delorme of Cadyville, New York. Mrs. Delorme learned this ballad
from her father.

M. Olney, Marjorie Porter, Collectors
December 4, 1941

THE DEWY DENS OF DARROW
(Child 214)

Now a father had a young ploughboy,
Whom this lady loved most dearly;
She dressed him as a galliant knight
To fight for her on Darrow.

Then he went up this high, high hill,
And on the lane so narrow,
And there he saw nine noble knights
On the Dewy Dens of Darrow.

"O it's will you try the hunting hound?
Or will you try the arrow?
Or will you try the single sword
On the Dewy Dens of Darrow?"

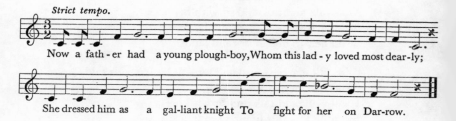

Strict tempo.

Now a fath-er had a young plough-boy, Whom this lad-y loved most dear-ly;

She dressed him as a gal-liant knight To fight for her on Dar-row.

"No, I won't try the hunting hound,
Nor will I try the arrow,
But I will try the single sword
On the Dewy Dens of Darrow."

His sword he drew—three knights he slew,
And was fighting with the other,
When her brother sprang from behind a tree
And they shot him with their arrow.

And she went up this high, high hill,
And on the lane so narrow,
And there she saw her noble knight
On the Dewy Dens of Darrow.

Her hair was about three-quarters long,
And the color being yellow,
She tied it round his waist so strong,
And she carried him home to Darrow.

"O daughter, dear, dry up those tears,
And give no more to sorrow,
For tomorrow you'll wed with a handsomer knight
Than the one you lost on Darrow."

"O father, dear, you have nine sons,
And you may wed them all tomorrow;
But you'll never find a handsomer knight,
Than the one I lost on Darrow."

As sung by Mrs. Lily Delorme of Cadyville, New York.

M. Olney, Marjorie Porter, Collectors
December 4, 1941

YOUNG JOHNNY OF HAZELGREEN
(Child 293)

"O, what is the matter my pretty fair maid,
What makes you sigh and moan?
Your father is dead and your mother's alive,
I dare you not go home."
"My father is dead and my mother's alive
But I value it not a pin,
I am weeping for my own true love,
Young Johnny of Hazelgreen."

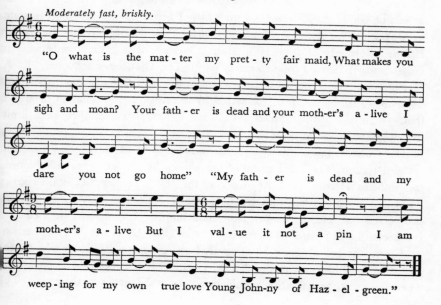

"O what is the mat-ter my pret-ty fair maid, What makes you sigh and moan? Your fath-er is dead and your moth-er's a-live I dare you not go home" "My fath-er is dead and my moth-er's a-live But I val-ue it not a pin I am weep-ing for my own true love Young John-ny of Haz-el-green."

"Come, go with me, my pretty fair maid,
Come go along with me,
And I'll take you to as fine a lord
As ever you wish to see."
And when they came to the castle-gate,
Such a crowd there ne'er was seen,
And amongst the crowd was her own true love,
Young Johnny of Hazelgreen.

"You're welcome back, dear father," he said,
"You're welcome back to me.
You've brought me back my bonny fair bride,
I thought I never should see."
For twenty-five kisses he gave to her
Before he let her in, saying,
"I hope you'll make a virtuous bride
For Johnny of Hazelgreen."

. . . For instance, there is a most exciting moment in history well told in the
annals of Gloucester, Massachusetts, which I have never come upon in song,
in Massachusetts. But it was sung in Orford, New Hampshire, by Mr. Albert
Howard, formerly of Blue Hill, Maine. I doubt if it is commonly sung in
Guysborough, Nova Scotia. This is why: The Gloucester schooner "E. A.
Horton" was taken into custody by the Dominion of Canada about the 1st of
September, 1871 (not 1861, as stated by the singer), for violation of an old
treaty requiring United States fishermen to stay outside a three-mile limit.
The seized ship was moored and dismantled at a wharf in Guysborough, Nova
Scotia. Already, under flimsy pretexts, other ships had been seized and held
without redress. The government of the United States had repeatedly ignored
the problem. Hence one of the owners of the "E. A. Horton," Captain Harvey
Knowlton, took matters into his own hands. Earlier in his career, he had
prospected for gold in Alaska. This stood him in good stead. Disguised as a
prospector he appeared in Manchester, Nova Scotia, to obtain specimens of
gold from the region. Soon he discovered six American fishermen who volunteered to help him rescue the "E. A. Horton." They reckoned upon a time
when the moon and the tide should be most advantageous to their plan. The

narrow channel was "perched". (The Oxford Dictionary explains that in 1465, a perch was "a pole set up in the sea or river to serve as a mark for navigation.") By the grapevine method, Captain Knowlton learned where the sails, rigging, etc., were stored.

By Sunday, October 8, came a bright, starlit night and a favorable northwest breeze. In a nearby barn, six American sailors were hiding. Before midnight, Captain Knowlton was in a loft assembling what he thought were the appurtenances of the "E. A. Horton". Unfortunately he brought to the schooner sails belonging to some other boat. The delay of returning those and getting the right ones was serious. By the time they could be off, the ship was aground. Had anyone come to the wharf at that hour, it could have been serious! A warp was got out and the vessel hove astern. Not until 2:30 was she actually afloat. Then, according to a contemporary account published by George H. Proctor of Gloucester, she gave Guysborough a "clean pair of heels." Pursuit was expected and planned for. Captain Knowlton chose passage through the Little Canso towards the northern Gulf Stream, then across the southeast part of Georges Banks, direct for Cape Anne. The ship had been well stocked with water and provisions, but nautical instruments and charts were lacking. When upon the high seas, they weathered an easterly gale. All this is as preface to the song. I should add that "red ruin" was rum. Now here is the way the folks passed that news around in a tune:

As sung by Mr. Albert Howard in Orford, New Hampshire, formerly of Blue Hill, Maine.
M. Olney, Collector
November 18, 1942

THE SCHOONER E. A. HORTON

Come all you sons of Uncle Sam, come listen to me awhile,
And I'll tell you of a capture that was made in Yankee style.
'Twas the Schooner E. A. Horton in the British harbor lie,
She was shaken by the "Sweepstakes" while cruising in disguise.
Our treaties they've rejected and our governments defied.
It's now you've stole our fishermen so Johnnies, mind yer eye.

'Twas the thirteenth day of October in the year of sixty-one,
Brave Knowlton and his comrades, the day it was begun

While the British thick-skulls were sleepin' with red ruin on their brain
We stole away our fisherman and brought her back again.

Triumphantly.

Come, all you sons of Un - cle Sam, come list - en to me a - while,

And I'll tell you of a capt - ure that was made in Yan - kee style.

'Twas the Schoon-er "E. A. Hor - ton" in the Brit - ish har - bor lie
Our — treat-ies they've re - ject - ed and our gov - ern-ments de - fied.

She was tak - en by the "Sweep-stakes" while cruis-ing in dis - guise.
It's — now you've stole our fish-er - men so John-nies, mind yer eye.

Remaining verses:

'Twas the thir-teenth day of Oct - to - ber in the year six - ty - one.

Brave Knowl-ton and his com - rades the day it was be - gun

While the Brit - ish thick skulls were sleep - in' with red ru - in on their brain

We stole a - way our fish - er - man and brought her back a - gain.

Says brave Knowlton to his comrades, "If you will follow me
We'll have the Horton home again whate'er the cost may be,
We'll stick to one another like brothers just as true
And we'll show these Yankee thievish-men what Yankee lads can do."

'Twas early the next mornin' the news did spread about;
They found the gold prospector with the Horton had stepped out;
The news began to penetrate the British skulls so thick
They finally did acknowledge 'twas a bold and Yankee trick.

Now, boys, there is a jolly time in Glou-chester tonight,
For heavy guns are firin' and torches burnin' bright.
The band plays, "Yankee Doodle" and the voices loudly ring
For the Yankee boys are shoutin' that the Horton has got in.

Now you Dominion Canaday, I warn you to beware.
You better sign the treaty and settle this affair.
And always do to others as you'll have 'em do to you
And don't try to treat your neighbor like old Johnny tried to do.

Mr. Charles L. Cooke of Ripton, Vermont, "worded" this, at the age of 76, July 24, 1941, as sung by his mother, Mrs. Mary O. Tinum of Kennebunk, Maine, whose grandfather, Jeremiah Paul, "was a sea captain out of Kennebunk" of whom the song is sung.
H. H. F., Collector
July 24, 1941

CAP'N PAUL

'Twas in the month of September
In the month of September we hear
Brig Mariner sailed over the bar
From Kennebunk away she went
To the West Indies she was sent.

Seven men all dressed in seamen's suits
Did bid their native land adieu.
The watery ocean they did take
Expecting a safe port to make.

They had not sail-ed very long
Before there did a storm arise
Which put those men in sad surprise.

The Brig upset on the wide main
And drown-ed those unhappy men.
Six of them made the sea their grave
And tasted death beneath the waves.

The Captain with them did not drown
But as the Brig turned upside down
Under the bottom there was a piece
Which he caught hold of and held fast.

In this condition there he lay
The space of three whole nights and days
And when the sun went down at night
Oh, what a dark and gloomy sight!

Captain Rooch came on the leeward side.
'Twas Captain Paul he then espied.

*Mr. Cooke recalls no more but knows Captain Paul
was saved in the next verses.*

Another instance of the far flung ballad is in a song "In the Dense Woods"
known to Mrs. Abbie Burgess of Providence, Rhode Island. It retells the
tragedy of an old man wandering and dying near Jackson, New Hampshire.
Mrs. Burgess learned a fragment sung in Jackson, New Hampshire, by Mr.
Damon Chesley. She spoke of him as an old farmer who used to weave and
sing at the same time. The song was about an uncle of Si Gale, the proprietor
of the Eagle Mountain House. "This uncle whose name I do not know, was
lost in the woods. They looked for him for many days, and he was found dead
in the snow." From Plymouth, Massachusetts, a descendant in the family,
Mr. George E. Gale, wrote, "There was no snow to track him . . . only in one
place. He went out Sunday and was found the next Sunday. His mother
always claimed he died on Friday morning. I knew some of the men that
found him and they said he died of hunger and grief. I don't think he froze
to death."

H. H. F., Collector
January, 1945

IN THE DENSE WOODS

(The death of James Fernald. Died in the year 1860.)

In the dense woods alone I roam
Away from friends and far from home.
I see no signs my heart to cheer.
No human voice can I hear.

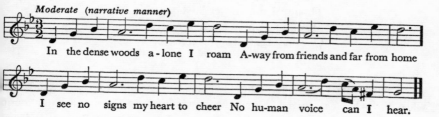

Oh, I am lost, my God, 'tis true,
Lost from my friends and human view,
And here I must remain
And never see my home again.

The cold wet ground must be my bed
While gushing tears I here do shed.
The tempest howls, the rain descends.
Oh, Jesus, must my life here end?

I start, I haste, I travel on,
But soon I to this spot return.
I'll strive from here my steps to trace,
No longer stay in this dreary place.

Weary and cold and hungry, too,
I weep, I sigh, for oh, I know I am lost,
And here I sure must die
While through the trees the winds do sigh.

And icy coldness o'er me steals
And death-like stupor now I feel.
I sink, I fall to rise no more.
The conflict past, my life is o'er.

Farewell, dear Mother, I am gone
While you are left on earth to mourn.
Farewell to Sister and Brothers dear;
Farewell to woods and waters here.

I hope God's mercy will me save
Though I may never have a grave.
May Jesus Christ my soul receive;
Oh, may I in His presence live.

. . . I have talked with people now living who as children were on the beach when the schooner arrived. Fireworks, gun salutes, speeches and band music were better than "beating the bounds" to assist memories. But never in its locale, only in New Hampshire have we come upon the way the people *sang* of the events.

Also, far from the sea in Ripton on Bread Loaf Mountain in Vermont, we recorded a song "Captain Paul" which never in the region of Kennebunk, Maine, has been recovered. But the singer's grandfather "a sea captain out of Kennebunk" was Jeremiah Paul, the hero of the wrecked brig.

It is interesting to note how altered from the original poem are the folk lines, found in Rhode Island. There was always a "t" in the folk version.

Contributed by mail by Mr. George E. Gale, 3 Bay View Avenue, Plymouth, Massachusetts. As sung by Mrs. Abbey Burgess of Providence, Rhode Island and North Conway New Hampshire.

H. H. F., Collector
January, 1945

In the denst woods alone I roam
Remote from friends and far from home.
No human voices can I hear;
No knowing sounds my heart to cheer.

And am I lost? My God, it's true

....

....

....

I start, I rove, each way I turn
But soon I to this place return.
I'll strive from here my steps to trace,
No longer stay in this drear place.

Farewell to brothers, sisters, friend;
My earthly days are at an end.
Farewell to mother, father, too;
I'll soon be lost to human view.

This could easily have been only a collection of ballads with tunes. It tends, however, to be more comprehensive, to show the lure and the zest or the unknown at every turn of the road or on any doorstone in New ngland. It should share, where possible, the storied origins of a ballad . . . rtainly its latest reincarnation. That word comes naturally—"in carni" eaning "in the flesh." For the latest singer is the current life-blood of the llad.

A book seems little enough unless one senses the author. This book will seem tle enough unless innumerable authors come alive within its pages.

INDEX OF TITLES

*A number in parentheses following the title refers to the ballad
identification system devised by the late Francis James Child.*